The LSB and Other
Unusual Bible Questions

Dr. Steve Combs

Published in the USA by
The Old Paths Publications
www.theoldpathspublications.com

Published in the USA by
The Old Paths Publications
www.theoldpathspublications.com

Copyright © 2022 by Steve Combs

ISBN: **979-8-9857165-5-9**

The Author may be contacted by writing:
bpsg.scombs@gmail.org

English Bible quotations in this book are from the King James Version, unless otherwise identified. This author considers the KJV to be completely accurate and the Word of God in the English language.

Cover Photo background Great Isaiah Scroll
QIsa example of damage col 12-13.jpg
Wikipedia Public Domain jb344tul

Global Bible Translators
www.bpsglobal.org

Table of Contents

Chapter 1: What is the LSB? 7

The NASB Legacy 9

Distinctives of the LSB 19

Chapter 2: Is God's Name in Hebrew Yahweh or Jehovah? 21

God's Name 22

The Modern Doctrine of the Hebrew Name of God 26

The LSB Stand 26

How is the Name of God Pronounced? 27

The Use of Adonai... 29

The Witness of Vav 36

Transliteration in European Translations 38

The Hebrew Language 39

Yahweh, a Horrifying Connection 41

The LSB Old Testament Disconnect 47

Chapter 3: How Should God's Name be Translated 49

How God Translated His Name.. 49

How Should We Translate His Name? 51

Principle 1: Choose a Name from the Native Culture 52

Principle 2: Contextual Conditioning 59

Chapter 4: Should Δοῦλος (Doulos) be translated Servant or Slave 63

Definitions.. 64

Slavery in the Roman Empire 67

What Saith the Scriptures?... 68

Is a Christian Servant a Slave? 71

About the Author... 75

Notes... 76

Dedication

This volume is dedicated to my precious, beloved wife, Suzanne, who gives me strength and encouragement and wisdom. She has stood by me for many years in spite of my many faults and failures. She has helped me get up when I fall and advised me on how to keep going. God knew what He was doing when He gave her to me.

Other Books written by the Author

The Fellowship of the Mystery: The Book of Ephesians
The Power of the Gospel: The Book of Romans
A Practical Theology of Bible Translating
The Translator's Grammar of the Textus Receptus
Election and Predestination
Every Word to Every People
Regions Beyond: The Task of Missions in the Twenty-First Century

Books Edited by the Author

The Greek New Testament
The Parallel Greek-English KJV New Testament

Chapter One
What is the LSB?

Recently I received a communication from a friend asking me about John MacArthur's new Bible translation. This was a surprising question, because John MacArthur is not a Bible translator. Nevertheless, I learned that he was the prime mover of a new Bible translation. So, we must answer the questions, "What is the LSB," and "What has it done to the name of God?" Before we do, let's get a bit of information about John MacArthur for those who do not know him.

John MacArthur was born June 19, 1939. He attended Bob Jones University from 1957 to 1959. He graduated with a Master of Divinity degree in 1963 from The Bible Institute of Los Angeles' new Talbot Theological Seminary in La Mirada, California. He received an honorary Doctor of Divinity degree from Grace Graduate School in 1976 and from Talbot Theological Seminary in 1977. In 1964, he began to serve as associate pastor of Harry MacArthur Memorial Bible Church under his father, Jack MacArthur, the senior pastor. This church later changed its name to Calvary Bible Church and is in Burbank, California. In 1969, he was made senior pastor of Grace Community Church in Sun Valley, California, where he is still the pastor. Since 1977, he has spoken on the international radio program, *Grace to You*. In 1985, he became president of Master's University and in 1989 he was made president of the newly created Master's Seminary.[1]

John MacArthur announced a new translation project in April 2020. MacArthur's favorite version of the Bible has long been the New American Standard Bible. The new translation is a revision of the NASB and the translators are professors at Master's University and Master's Seminary. The new translation is called *The Legacy Standard Version*. John MacArthur believes the NASB was the most accurate translation in English and the Legacy Standard Version (LSB) would make it even more accurate. That was his stated goal. Let's permit John MacArthur himself tell us about it.

> We're just grateful to the Lord. Today, I did something really unusual. Something that is not only

unusual for me but is unusual... I've never heard of anything like this.

As you know for, well, half a century, I've taught the word of God and I've always preached from the New American Standard Bible, the most accurate English translation. We have been given a gift, and that is we have been given the opportunity to take the New American Standard Bible, and to be licensed to do a translation work that will make that translation even more accurate.

Who's going to do that? Well, Dr. Abner Chou, who heads up the biblical studies department at The Master's University, and Will Varner, New Testament scholar, Jason Beals, another scholar, linguist from the University, and then from the Seminary, Joe Zhakevich, who is an Old Testament scholar, Harvard-trained in Hebrew and Semitic languages. Mark [Zhakevich] who's trained in New Testament Greek, and Paul Twiss. All six of these guys are going through the Hebrew and the Greek of the entire Bible, tightening this into a... can I say it this way... an already accurate, but more refined translation from the original Hebrew and the original Greek.

And it's basically driven toward two things: one is even greater accuracy and the other is greater consistency. This is an incredible thing that they're doing. I'm amazed at the work they're doing. I've seen some of it. What's going to come out of this is a new edition called the Legacy Standard Bible.

It's going to be the expositor's dream Bible, to have the absolutely accurate, consistent text to study, to preach, and it's... it's bound to be the most accurate, the most consistent, translation in English, and that is a gift to the church. And the Lockman Foundation that did the original work on the NASB has given us the opportunity to do that. So it's our men from the

University and the Seminary who're doing this refining translation. [2]

The NASB Legacy

The Legacy Standard Bible now has a web site, www.lsbible.org. According to the web site, one of the purposes of the LSB is to preserve the legacy of the NASB.

> The Legacy Standard Bible is a translation that— at its core—seeks to be a window into the original Hebrew, Aramaic, and Greek. By translating individual words as consistently as possible within their various nuances, it allows the reader to discern the Author's intent. In this way, the refinements in the LSB also preserve the legacy of the NASB. [3]

On the web site you can read the preface to the LSB and the Text of the LSB beginning in Genesis 1. The preface lists several goals of the LSB. Among them are the following.

> 1. ... "to uphold the style and translational choices of the NASB as much as possible."
> 2. ... "it has endeavored to follow through on the NASB's stated intent to be true to the original Hebrew, Aramaic, and Greek ... the goal of this translation is to be a window into the original text."
> 3. "Within that goal, this revision has focused upon accuracy and consistency." [4]

Basically, this new version is a warmed up and rebooted new New American Standard with a few changes in wording. Otherwise, it is the same NASB as the old New American Standard. If you caught it, they want this version to be a window into the "original text." They did not say the original *language*, but, rather, the original *text*. What do they mean by this? They could not mean *original* text, could they? The original writings are the first writings, and they no longer exist. The translator's explain what they mean later in the preface, and it is *not* the *original* text.

> The Legacy Standard Bible utilizes the latest edition of Rudolf Kittel's Biblia Hebraica together with the most recent light from lexicography, cognate languages, and the Dead Sea Scrolls ... The Legacy Standard Bible has the benefit of a number of critical Greek texts in determining the best variant reading to translate. The 27th edition of Eberhard Nestle's Novum Testamentum Graece, supplemented by the 28th edition in the General Epistles, serve as the base text. On every variant reading the Society of Biblical Literature GNT as well as the Tyndale House GNT were also consulted. [5]

So, the Old Testament of the LSB came primarily from Biblia Hebraica, which was developed by Rudolph Kittel and first published in 1906. The basis for this first edition was the Second Rabbinical Bible of Jacob Ben Chayim, published in 1524/1525 by Daniel Bomberg. Over the next several centuries, the Ben Chayim OT was universally recognized as the definitive Hebrew text. The KJV translators used it as the basis of the King James Version.[6] The second edition of Biblia Hebraica was published in 1913 with only slight differences from the first edition. [7]

However, the textual basis was different for the third edition of Biblia Hebraica, published in 1937. It abandoned the Ben Chayim text and used the Hebrew Leningrad manuscript as the basis of the text. The Leningrad manuscript is dated about 1008 AD. It is said to be a "Ben Asher" text and to have many similarities to the Ben Chayim text.

However, the third edition is not the current edition in use today. Editions after the third edition became known as Biblia Hebraica Stuttgartensia and have been replaced since 2004 with the Biblia Hebraica Quinta. The Stuttgartensia incorporated variants from other sources, especially the Dead Sea Scrolls. The Quinta extends these variations further. The preface to the LSB does not make it clear which of these editions is in view by the statement "the latest edition of Rudolf Kittel's Biblia Hebraica." However, even if it is the third edition of Biblia Hebraica, which is the Leningrad manuscript, it is clear that the basis of the OT translation is not Ben Chayim and, therefore, not the same as the KJV. It is also clear that the LSB basis of OT translation goes beyond the

Hebrew text to the Dead Sea Scrolls and other sources, which can easily cause more variations from the KJV.

For the New Testament, the "27th edition of Eberhard Nestle's Novum Testamentum Graece, supplemented by the 28th edition in the General Epistles, serve as the base text." This was also supplemented by several other Greek texts. The Nestle text used to be called the Nestle-Aland text because Kurt Aland helped edit it. Kurt Aland was also involved in editing the United Bible Societies Greek text. The UBS Greek text is in its 5th edition (2014) and the Nestle text is now in its 28th edition (2012). Both Greek New Testaments have an identical text. [8]

The Nestle and UBS Texts differ greatly from the Received Greek Text, from which the KJV was translated. There are thousands of word differences between them. Everett W. Fowler evaluated the third edition of the UBS Greek Text compared to the Received Text, which, as mentioned before, is the same text as the Nestle from the 26th through the 28th edition. He published the results in *Evaluating Versions of the New Testament*.[9] Figure 1 enumerates the whole verses and partial verses missing from the UBS text as compared to the TR.

Number of whole verses missing in UBS	17
Omissions of whole and partial verses	1309

Fig. 1

The total word differences were categorized as follows. These do not include differences in spelling of proper nouns. The category of "words classed as different words" does not include "spelling variations shown in Greek lexicons as accepted ways of spelling words which have identical meanings, but which are not listed as different words (for example: labor=labour)."

Words in the Received Text omitted from UBS	3602
Words classed as different words	3146
Words in UBS not in the Received Text	976
Words spelled different, but not different words	950
Total word differences	8674

Fig. 2

Why do we have such concern over individual words, even if some of them do not materially affect the translation? There are a total of 8,674 word differences between the Received Greek Text and the Nestle/UBS Greek Text. The New Testament was inspired in Greek and every Word of God is important. God, Himself, emphasizes the importance of every word. Either the Nestle Text is the Word of God or the Received Text is. They cannot both be His Word.

Therefore, based on the basic texts used for translating the NASB and the revision of it, the LSB, there should be serious errors in the English Bible text. Indeed, there is. In fact, the majority of the errors in the old New American Standard are present in the new Legacy Standard Version. Below is a list of some of the more serious errors. These are only a few of the many problems of the LSB New Testament text and they should be viewed as categories of errors, because the errors are many.

1.   Matthew 1:2

LSB: Abraham **was the father of** Isaac, and Isaac **was the father of** Jacob
KJV: Abraham **begat** Isaac; and Isaac **begat** Jacob;
Comment: The translations "was the father of" and "begat" are both from the same Greek word, ἐγέννησε (egennese), which is a form of the word, γεννάω (gennao). According to Thayer, γεννάω, means "of men who fathered children: to be born, to be begotten." [10] In other words, it means to give birth to. Strong's defines it "to procreate." [11] The translation "was the father of" is not a literal translation of the word. "Begat" is literal. The way the LSB rendered the Greek word is what we would call an English idiomatic translation. Unfortunately, it is not an idiomatic phrase that is very close to the meaning of the Greek word. The word in Greek, γεννάω, means to physically give birth to someone, that is, to be a person's biological parent. We all know that, in English, to be someone's father does not always mean to be that person's biological father. You can be a stepfather or an adoptive father. Therefore, "was the father of" is not a very good translation. But, this is just the beginning of woes.

2.   Matthew 1:25

LSB: but kept her a virgin until she gave birth to a Son; and he called His name Jesus

KJV: And knew her not till she had brought forth her **firstborn** son: and he called his name JESUS.

Comment: The LSB leaves out the theologically important word "firstborn." They also added the word "virgin," which isn't even *in their* Greek text. The KJV translated this sentence literally, but the LSB translated it idiomatically, in this case showing that the LSB is *not* an accurate translation. They used a method known as *dynamic equivalence*, which allows translators to use whatever words they think are necessary, whether or not they are in or implied by their Greek text.

3.   Matthew 5:22

LSB: But I say to you that everyone who is angry with his brother shall be guilty before the court

KJV: But I say unto you, That whosoever is angry with his brother **without a cause** shall be in danger of the judgment

Comment: The LSB leaves out the phrase "without a cause." Since Jesus Christ did get angry at his Jewish brethren, this omission judges Jesus Christ as a guilty sinner!

4.   Matthew 5:44

LSB: But I say to you, love your enemies and pray for those who persecute you

KJV: But I say unto you, Love your enemies, **bless them that curse you, do good to them that hate you,** and pray for them which **despitefully use you, and** persecute you;

Comment: The LSB leaves out the whole highlighted section.

5.   Matthew 12:6

LSB: But I say to you that **something** greater than the temple is here.

KJV: But I say unto you, That in this place is *one* greater than the temple.

Comment: The words *something* and *one* in these verses are not in the Greek text.

1. The KJV puts the word *one* in italics to indicate that it is not in the Greek text, but the LSB leaves the word *something* in normal type.

2. The Nestle and the TR basically read the same in this verse. The KJV translators inserted the word *one*, so that the reader would understand that it refers to Christ. The LSB inserts the word *something* referring to ... what? Does this reveal something about the LSB (or NASB) translator's view of Christ?

3. The Greek text reads this way, "But I say to you, that a greater than the temple is in this place." The word μεῖζων (meizon), a greater, is an adjective. Adjectives in Greek describe nouns, just as they do in English. What noun does this word describe? To help identify the noun being described, we must look for a noun that matches the grammar of the adjective. Mezon in Greek is Nominative case, singular number, and masculine gender. What other word matches this in the context? There is a word in verse 8, Son. This is the only word that matches the adjective in grammar in the immediate context. Therefore, the Greek, μεῖζων, "a greater," refers to Jesus, and it is accurate to insert the word *one*, referring to a *person*. The translation *something* is an insult to the Lord Jesus Christ. But, insulting the Lord Jesus is something the LSB excels at. Moreover, the Greek word is masculine gender, so it is not referring to some *thing*. It is referring to *some man*.

6.   Matthew 17:21

LSB: [But this kind does not go out except by prayer and fasting."]
KJB: Howbeit this kind goeth not out but by prayer and fasting.
Comment: the LSB puts this verse in brackets implying it should not be there. It puts doubt in the mind of the reader that the verse is truly inspired. This make the verse entirely ineffective

in the minds of some, because the Word of God requires faith to be effective (1 Thess. 2:13). Matthew 8:11; 23:14; Mark 7:16; 9:44, 46; 11:26; 15:28; 16:9-20; Lk. 17:36; 23:37; John 5:4; 7:53-8:11; Acts 8:37; 15:34 are also bracketed.

7.   Matthew 27:35

LSB: And when they had crucified Him, they divided up His garments among themselves by casting lots.
KJV: And they crucified him, and parted his garments, casting lots: **that it might be fulfilled which was spoken by the prophet, They parted my garments among them, and upon my vesture did they cast lots.**
Comments: The entire phrase is omitted, hiding from God's people that the event is a fulfillment of prophecy.

8.   Mark 1:2, 3

LSB: As it is written in Isaiah the prophet:
"Behold, I send My messenger ahead of You,
Who will prepare Your way; The voice of one crying in the wilderness, 'Make ready the way of the Lord,
Make His paths straight.'"
KJV: As it is written in the prophets, Behold, I send my messenger before thy face, which shall prepare thy way before thee. The voice of one crying in the wilderness, Prepare ye the way of the Lord, make his paths straight.
Comment: The LSB comment that the quotes here are from Isaiah the prophet is an open lie. The quotes are from both Isaiah and Malachi (Mal. 3:1; Is. 40:3). The KJV gets it right by attributing the quotes to "the prophets."

9.   Mark 16:9-20 are in brackets in the LSB and an alternative short ending is given after that, also placed in brackets. "[*And they promptly reported all these instructions to Peter and his companions. And after that, Jesus Himself sent out through them from east to west the sacred and imperishable preaching of eternal salvation.*]" The KJV has no brackets and omits the short ending. This short ending is in a strange style and vocabulary compared to the rest of the Book of Mark.

10.   Luke 1:28

LSB: And coming in, he said to her, "Greetings, favored one! The Lord *is* with you."
KJV: And the angel came in unto her, and said, Hail, thou that art highly favoured, the Lord is with thee: **blessed art thou among women.**
Comment: The marked phrase is omitted in the LSB and the first part of the verse is altered and "the angel" is omitted.

11.   Luke 2:14

LSB: "Glory to God in the highest, And on earth peace **among men with whom He is pleased.**"
KJV: Glory to God in the highest, and on earth peace, **good will toward men.**
Comment: This verse is doctrinally significant. it deals with God's purpose in sending the Lord Jesus Christ to earth. These two marked translations come from the same basic Greek words, except that the word for good will, εὐδοκία, eudokia, is in the nominative case in the TR and in the genitive case in Nestle. Nevertheless, that difference does not justify the loose translation in the LSB. *The LSB wording is an interpretation, not a translation.* However, that is not the most important thing. What was God's purpose in sending Christ? Was it to bless good men with whom He is pleased? Is God really looking for men who are doing well so He can reward them for their goodness and good works? Or, did He send Christ because of *His* good will toward men? Did Christ come to bring the grace of God and the gift of eternal life to men who need it? Men do not earn salvation by works. They are given salvation by grace through faith. The importance of this verse is show that Christ came to give God's grace to sinners. "For the Son of man is come to seek and to save that which was lost" (Luke 19:10).

12.   Luke 2:33

LSB: And **His father** and mother were marveling at the things which were being said about Him.

KJV: And **Joseph** and his mother marvelled at those things which were spoken of him.

Comment: Joseph was not Jesus' true father, yet the LSB says that he was. The KJV acknowledges his true origin, God. This verse is also doctrinally important.

13.   Luke 23:38

LSB: Now there was also an inscription above Him, "THIS IS THE KING OF THE JEWS."

KJV: And a superscription also **was written over him in letters of Greek, and Latin, and Hebrew**, THIS IS THE KING OF THE JEWS.

Comment: The highlighted words are omitted in the LSB. This is significant, in that, these words can be used to prove that Jesus' language on earth was Hebrew, not Aramaic.

14.   John 1:18

LSB: No one has seen God at any time; **the only begotten God** who is in the bosom of the Father, He has explained *Him*.

KJV: No man hath seen God at any time; **the only begotten Son**, which is in the bosom of the Father, he hath declared him.

Comment: The difference between the highlighted phrases is very significant. Was Jesus truly a begotten God? Did God the Father bring Him into existence sometime in eternity past? If God begat Jesus as God, doesn't that make Him a lesser god than the Father? Doesn't that also mean He is separate from the Father and that the Godhead is really three Gods? Doesn't that make us polytheists? Aren't the Russellites (the JW's) right after all? [12] The LSB reading is heresy of the grossest sort.

15.   Acts 9:6

LSB: but rise up and enter the city, and it will be told you what you must do.

KJV: **And he trembling and astonished said, Lord, what wilt thou have me to do? And the Lord said unto him,** Arise, and go into the city, and it shall be told thee what thou must do.

Comment: The entire marked portion is omitted in the LSB. The omission of the portion hides the change in Paul's attitude. This is an illustration of man's repentance before God; a change of heart from "I will do what I want to do" to "Lord, what will you have me do?"

16.   Acts 9:29

LSB: And he was talking and arguing with the Hellenistic *Jews*, but they were attempting to put him to death.
KJV: And he spake boldly **in the name of the Lord Jesus**, and disputed against the Grecians: but they went about to slay him.
Comments: The LSB omits the highlighted portion. There are many verses where the LSB omits or puts in italics the name of the Lord. When the LSB puts a word in italics it is saying to the reader that it is doubtful that the word is in the original text. In these same verses the KJV includes the name of the Lord and does not put it in italics, because the word is found in the Textus Receptus.

17.   1 John 5:7

LSB: For there are three that bear witness:
KJV: For there are three that bear record **in heaven, the Father, the Word, and the Holy Ghost: and these three are one.**
Comment: The LSB omits the highlighted words. 1 John 5:7 is the greatest and clearest verse in the New Testament on the Trinity. Therefore, it is the most attacked verse in the New Testament. All popular modern versions attack these words. This includes the NKJV which casts doubt on the verse in a footnote. For an extended discussion see the authors book, *A Practical Theology of Bible Translating*, available from The Old Paths Publications.

These few examples will hopefully be enough to show the reader that the LSB is merely one more modern version that is built on corrupted copies of the original language texts. A great deal more could be added to this list. The last half of Romans 8:1 is omitted, the blood is missing from Colossians 1:14, Christ is omitted in 1 Cor. 9:1, 18 and other places, Jesus is omitted in 2 Cor 5:18 and other places, Lord is omitted in

2 Cor. 4:10 and other places, and so on with many omissions and additions. You can find a good guide to check this and other versions on the web site for Global Bible Translators, www.bpsglobal.org/information-for-translators.html.

Distinctives of the LSB

The LSB boasts two unusual distinctives. One is that they profess to consistently translate the Greek word, δοῦλος, doulos, as *slave*, rather than as *servant* like the KJV does. They explain this in the preface to the LSB.

> The NASB has already translated the Greek term doulos frequently as "slave" in the NT. The LSB made this consistent across the NT. This upholds the lexical definition of the term, its consistent translation, and its distinction from other terms that do denote a "servant." Such consistency also highlights a biblical theological reality that Christians were slaves of sin but now are slaves of Christ (Rom 6:16–22). Biblical writers did not shy from this term because it condemned a wicked form of slavery (i.e., to sin, Satan, and death), highlighted the power of redemption, and affirmed one's total submission to the lordship of Christ.[13]

The KJV translates δοῦλος as *servant*, *bond*, or *bondman*. John MacArthur and the translators of the LSB seem to believe that to translate this word as *servant* is an error. In a later chapter, we will take an in depth look at that question. We will find that the question is far less simple than that. There are more aspects to it. Slaves in the Roman Empire were captive bondmen with no free will. Do Christian servants fit the profile of a slave in the Roman Empire? We shall see in chapter four.

The other LSB distinctive has to do with the name of God in the Old Testament. The KJV translates the name Jehovah as LORD almost every time it is used in the Old Testament. The LSB has dispensed with LORD and uses the Hebrew name; or so they say. They say it is Yahweh rather than Jehovah. The LSB retains the English name for other Hebrew names of God. They do not transliterate the Hebrew name as they do for Jehovah. *Elohim* is translated *God*. *Adonai* is translated *Lord* and so on. Let's allow the LSB to speak for itself.

> In the Scriptures, the name of God is significant and understandably so. Traditionally, the translation "God" renders the Hebrew word Elohim. Likewise, the word "Lord" is a translation of Adonai. In the LSB, God's covenant name is rendered as Yahweh. The meaning and implication of this name is God's self-deriving, ongoing, and never-ending existence. Exodus 3:14–15 shows that God Himself considered it important for His people to know His name. The effect of revealing God's name is His distinction from other gods and His expression of intimacy with the nation of Israel. Such a dynamic is a prevalent characteristic of the Scriptures as Yahweh appears in the OT over 6,800 times. [14]

It may seem reasonable to many to use the Hebrew name for the LORD in an English translation, rather than the traditional English name, LORD. The wonderful Hebrew name for the Lord God is made known to English speakers through Exodus 6:1-4. Nevertheless, putting the Hebrew name into English letters is not translating. When a foreign word is taken directly into another language in letters of the receiving language's alphabet, it is called transliterating. But, it not *translating*. Beyond that issue, there is another and greater issue. Is God's Hebrew name Yahweh or Jehovah? Which is the right pronunciation? This is a very controversial and complicated subject. We will investigate these issues in the next chapter.

Chapter Two
Is God's Name in Hebrew Yahweh or Jehovah?

There is a great disagreement on how the Hebrew name of God should be pronounced. The Hebrew alphabet only has consonants, no vowels. When words are pronounced, vowels are used, but the Hebrew alphabet itself contains no vowels. The vowel sounds are kept in memory. A Jewish child learns how to speak by listening. In school, children learn proper spelling of words and how those words are pronounced, so that when he sees a word he knows how it is spoken. Someone who has learned English from a child can do the same thing. For example, read ths sntnc: Gd blss yu.

In 70 AD, the Romans destroyed the temple and the city of Jerusalem. Up to that time, a standard copy of the Old Testament had been kept in the Temple. Since the Temple was destroyed, groups of scribes kept the Scriptures safe and preserved the traditional pronunciation of the words. A group of scribes known as the Masoretic Scribes worked from about the 6th century to the 11th century to preserve the Old Testament and the traditions related to it, including how the words are pronounced. They kept these traditions in a set of notes called the Masorah. By the 9th century they had developed a system of vowels to preserve the Biblical pronunciation in a written form. They wrote these vowels as a system of dots and dashes that are still used today.

I know there are some who believe the vowel points were a part of Hebrew when the Scriptures were given starting by about 1450 BC and that they are inspired. For purposes of this study, I have chosen to accept the traditional view, since the question has little bearing on the issues in this chapter.

Fig. 1

Nevertheless, the fact is that currently the Hebrew alphabet only has consonants. The vowel points are not considered to be part of the alphabet. Often publications in Israel (see the above issue of Epoch Times in Fig. 1) have no vowels. This has been true for centuries.

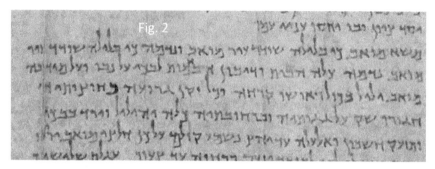

Fig. 2 shows the Great Isaiah Scroll from the Dead Sea Scrolls, no. 1QIsaᵃ, estimated date 100 BC. [15] There are no vowel points. Clearly, this is how Hebrew was written at that time.

Fig. 3 [16], opposite, is the Gezer Calendar written in archaic Hebrew letters. It is dated 10th century BC. Archaic Hebrew was also an alphabet with all consonants and this example indicates no vowel points.

God's Name

God speaks of His name is Exodus 6:3, 13, 14

And I appeared unto Abraham, unto Isaac, and unto Jacob, by the name of God Almighty, but by my name JEHOVAH was I not known to them ... And God said unto Moses, I AM THAT I AM: and he said, Thus shalt thou say unto the children of Israel, I AM hath sent me unto you. And God said moreover unto Moses, Thus shalt thou say unto the children of Israel, The LORD God of your fathers, the God of Abraham, the God of Isaac, and the God of Jacob, hath sent me unto you: this is my name for ever, and this is my memorial unto all generations.

God's name, Jehovah, is spelled in Hebrew with four consonants, written below. Hebrew is written right to left.

יהוה spelled, yod-Hey-vav-hey

When the vowel points supplied by the Masoretic scribes are written with this name, it looks like this.

יְהֹוָה transliterated Yehovah.

In reverse order, the vowels are ⃛ ⃛ and the vowels mean the following: e, o, and a. The first *consonant* of the name of God is pronounced like a y, the second like an h, the third like a v, and the last is like an h, which is silent at the end of a word. So, if you put all the letters and vowel points together you get Y-e-h-o-v-a-h or as it is in the KJV, *Jehovah*. In the early modern English of 1611, the letter J was pronounced like a y. If you look in a copy of the Hebrew Old Testament from which the KJV was translated, you will find the name written with the vowels exactly as it is above. Scholars call the Hebrew consonantal name the *tetragrammaton*, meaning four letters. We will call it *the name of God*.

This would seem to settle the question, would it not? Not at all. It is only the beginning of the controversy. This is a matter of great disagreement. During the Reformation (1500-1700), most Bible teachers believed the proper way the pronounce the name was Yehovah or Jehovah. However, today most Hebrew scholars and some Jewish Rabbis insist that Jehovah is *not* the correct way to pronounce the name. Many of them say it should be pronounced Yahweh. This all begins with a story. That story is below and all the scholars of the Yahweh opinion seem to be in agreement and many who accept the name as Jehovah swallow the story too, although some may suggest a different time in history when the Jewish practice mentioned began.

Probably the early Israelites actually pronounced the name Yahweh. But by the end of the pre-Christian era, a fear of misusing God's name developed (based on Exodus 20:7; Deuteronomy 5:11) to such a degree that pious Jews avoided speaking the divine name out loud. When it appeared in the Hebrew Scriptures read in the synagogue, they would substitute the word "adon or "adonay, meaning "lord, master"...To this day, orthodox Jews avoid even spelling God, and render it G-d out of reverence. They refer to YHWH as the Ineffable Name, the Unutterable Name or the Distinctive Name. The first step in the transition from Yahweh to Jehovah was the substitution of Adonai for Yahweh when the Scripture was read. [17]

This story is generally known and accepted, although some add one thing or another to it. An example of something added is found in the quote below. The story is that the Jews would not *speak* the name. Rather, when they came to the name, יהוה, they would speak Adonai or Adon instead (meaning Lord). They did not remove or change the sacred name in the written Scriptures. They would merely speak a different word when they saw the name of God written in the text. Yet, according to many, this somehow morphed into a plan of the Jews to change the *written* name into something it was *not*. Thereby, corrupting their own Scriptures.

Dr. J. B. Rotherham states in the preface of his Bible concerning Jehovah: "Erroneously written and pronounced Jehovah, which is merely a combination of the sacred Tetragrammaton and the vowels in the Hebrew word for Lord, substituted by the Jews for JHVH, because they shrank from pronouncing The Name ...

The Encyclopedia Britannica (Micropedia, vol. 10) says:

"Yahweh-the personal name of the [EI] of the Israelites ...The Masoretes, Jewish biblical scholars of the Middle Ages, replaced the vowel signs that had appeared above or beneath the consonants of YHWH with the vowel signs of Adonai or of Elohim. Thus the artificial name Jehovah (YeHoWaH) came into being. Although Christian scholars after the Renaissance and

Reformation periods used the term Jehovah for YHWH, in the 19th and 20th centuries biblical scholars again began to use the form Yahweh, thus this pronunciation of the Tetragrammaton was never really lost. Greek transcriptions also indicate that YHWH should be pronounced Yahweh." [18]

The Masoretes *invented* the vowel pointing and these commentators are saying that there was a conspiracy of the Rabbis and scribes to hide the name of God, so that they would be prevented from speaking it in vain. There are Jews today who also believe this. The web site, Hebrew 4 Christians, says this about the name of God.

> The Third Commandment (Exodus 20:7) states, "Thou shalt not take the name of the LORD thy God in vain; for the LORD will not hold him guiltless that taketh his name in vain." ... On account of this, the Masoretes ensured that the Name of the LORD would not be taken in vain by substituting the vowel marks for Adonai and putting them under the letters י-ה-ו-ה in the running text (this is called Qere ... [what is to be read] as opposed to Ketiv [what is to be written]). The Hebrew text, then, contains the Ketiv but uses the vowels of the Qere and this has led to the obviously incorrect pronunciation of the Name as "Jehovah" (in older English, "J" had a "y" sound). [19]

This same website had some comments about the alternative name embraced by many modern scholars and Jews, Yahweh.

> It was later speculated that perhaps the Masoretes reversed the vowels for Adonai when applied to the letters יהוה in the running text, so some attempted to "correct" the pronunciation by pronouncing the Name as "Yahoveh" or "Yahveh." This, too, is incorrect (though the construct form "Yah" probably is part of the original pronunciation (e.g., see Psalm 68:4; Isaiah 26:4)). Note that Yahweh is most

likely also an incorrect transliteration, since there is no "w" sound in Hebrew.[20]

The Modern Doctrine of the Hebrew Name of God

Modern Hebrew Scholars have built up a consistent narrative about what happened to the name of God and how it is to be pronounced. Below I have summarized the major points we have been taught so far.

    1.   The Jews developed a tradition of not speaking the sacred name of God. When they were reading the Scriptures and came to this name, they would say *Adon* or *Adonai*.

    2.   The Masoretic Scribes sought to keep the name from being desecrated by taking the vowel points of Adonai and applying them to the sacred name.

    3.   Because of this, the true pronunciation may be lost and the best pronunciation is Yahweh.

Is all this true? Is there historical evidence or other basis for teaching this? We will accept the first point to be true. This should be self-evident, because the Jews admit it and, even today, they practice this tradition. However, point two and three are open to debate. Point three depends on point two. So, is there historical evidence for point two? Is it real history or could it simply be a scholarly fantasy like the theory of Westcott and Hort that an official revision of the Greek New Testament took place in Syria in the 4th century, thereby producing the Byzantine or Traditional text type? The official revision theory has absolutely no historical evidence to confirm it. Likewise, I have searched for historical evidence to confirm point 2 and found none. All I have found are dogmatic assertions with no documentation.

The LSB Stand

The LSB translators and John MacArthur agreed to use Yahweh to transliterate the Sacred Name of the Lord, rather than translate it to LORD as the KJV did.

Names of God: In the Scriptures, the name of God is significant and understandably so. Traditionally, the translation "God" renders the Hebrew word Elohim. Likewise, the word "Lord" is a translation of Adonai. In the LSB, God's covenant name is rendered as Yahweh. The meaning and implication of this name is God's self-deriving, ongoing, and never-ending existence. Exodus 3:14–15 shows that God Himself considered it important for His people to know His name. The effect of revealing God's name is His distinction from other gods and His expression of intimacy with the nation of Israel. Such a dynamic is a prevalent characteristic of the Scriptures as Yahweh appears in the OT over 6,800 times. [21]

So, which is it? Is the name *Jehovah*, as it was generally accepted until the rise of the modern religious liberal movement in the 1800's? Or is it *Yahweh*, which is now generally accepted by liberal and evangelical scholars? At the outset of our investigation, let it be understood that neither Jehovah nor Yahweh are translations. Jehovah is a transliteration of the Hebrew name as it is generally found in Hebrew texts. A transliteration is taking the letters of a word in one language and putting them directly into letters of another language. For example, the Greek word for God is θεος and is transliterated into English as theos. Yahweh is a transliteration of יַהְוֶה.

How is the Name of God Pronounced?

It would be wise to address the third point first. Before spending time determining how to pronounce the name, we should know that God has not hidden it and it is not lost. To know that we have to go no further than the Scriptures themselves. We can know God's attitude about His name because He tells us.

And in very deed for this cause have I raised thee up, for to shew in thee my power; and that my name may be declared throughout all the earth. (Ex. 9:16)

My doctrine shall drop as the rain, my speech shall distil as the dew, as the small rain upon the tender herb, and as the showers upon the grass: Because I will publish the name of the LORD: ascribe ye greatness unto our God. (Deut. 32:2-3)

When a prophet speaketh in the name of the LORD, if the thing follow not, nor come to pass, that is the thing which the LORD hath not spoken, but the prophet hath spoken it presumptuously: thou shalt not be afraid of him. (Deuteronomy 18:22)

And the priests the sons of Levi shall come near; for them the LORD thy God hath chosen to minister unto him, and to bless in the name of the LORD; and by their word shall every controversy and every stroke be tried: (Deuteronomy 21:5)

And all people of the earth shall see that thou art called by the name of the LORD; and they shall be afraid of thee. (Deuteronomy 28:10)

Blessed be the LORD God, the God of Israel, who only doeth wondrous things. And blessed be his glorious name for ever: and let the whole earth be filled with his glory; Amen, and Amen. (Ps. 75:18, 19)

Therefore my people shall know my name: therefore they shall know in that day that I am he that doth speak: behold, it is I. (Isaiah 52:6)

Kings of the earth, and all people; princes, and all judges of the earth: 12 Both young men, and maidens; old men, and children: 13 Let them praise the name of the LORD: for his name alone is excellent; his glory is above the earth and heaven. 14 He also exalteth the horn of his people, the praise of all his saints; even of the children of Israel, a people near unto him. Praise ye the LORD. (Psalms 148:11-14)

God judged Pharaoh so that His name would be declared in all the earth. He wants His name published and greatness ascribed to Him. Prophets must speak in the name of the LORD. His servant must serve in the name of the LORD. God wanted all the people of the earth to know that Israel was called by His name. His name will be known and blessed forever. God has never hidden His name. His name has never been lost. He has preserved His name along with His word. It was known and is known and will be forever known.

The Use of Adonai

We have accepted the fact that the Jews *spoke* "Adon" or "Adonai" (which is the plural of Adon) when they saw the sacred name in the Scriptures. But, did they also write the vowels of Adonai in the sacred name to hide the true pronunciation? First, the historical evidence does not support this. That is not to say that they were unconcerned about the abuse of the sacred name. They did attempt to prevent the speaking of the name when the Scriptures were read, but not in this way. Before I reveal just what they did do, let's look closer at the question of whether they truly used the vowels of Adonai or Adon at all or not. Below is a comparison of the sacred name with Adon and Adonai with the vowel points. Pay careful attention to the vowel points. You do not need to know Hebrew to see the difference.

אֲדֹנָי	אָדוֹן	יְהֹוָה
Adonai	Adon	Yehovah

There are differences in these three words regarding the vowel points. Yehovah has three vowels, but Adon only has two. The sheva (:) at the beginning of Yehovah is sometimes silent, but it is pronounced with an e sound at the beginning of a word. Add to the fact that Adon has only two vowels, the further fact that those vowels are reversed in Yehovah. What about Adonai? It has three vowels like Yehovah, and the second two vowels are the same and in the same order as those in Yehovah. However, the first vowel in Adonai is *different* from the first vowel in Yehovah. The differences between these words tend *not* to support the assertion that the vowel points of Adon or Adonai were used in the sacred name.

Nevertheless, the Masoretic scribes apparently did have a plan to prevent the sacred name of God from being spoken. One can begin to see what they did from the very manuscript used as the basis of the Hebraica Stugartensia Old Testament and its successor, Biblia Hebraica Quinta. That is, the Leningrad Hebrew manuscript from 1008 AD. A portion from it is below showing how they wrote the sacred name.

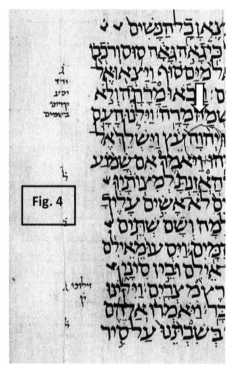

Fig. 4

The sacred name has four letters. Hebrew words start with a consonant. They are divided into syllables consisting of one or two consonants and a vowel making words in the following patterns CVCV or CVCVC or CVCCV or CVCCVC. The last pattern is what one may *think* he is seeing in the Leningrad manuscript [22] (Fig. 4 left) with the name of God being written YeHVaH. That is, with the middle vowel of Jehovah being absent. However, when the CVCCVC pattern appears, the final consonant in the first syllable, CVC, normally has a silent sheva (:) underneath it to show that it is the end of a syllable. This would be under the first Hey in God's name, thus, הַ. So, if we are really seeing the CVCCVC pattern, the last consonant of the first syllable, ה, should have a silent sheva beneath it, but there never is when this word appears with this spelling in ancient Hebrew manuscripts. The absence of a silent sheva indicates that there should be a vowel after the first Hey, ה. Therefore, this word exhibits a missing vowel. YeH?VaH is what we see. This makes the name unpronounceable in Hebrew.

So, when a reader encountered the name and saw that he could not pronounce it, he was reminded to substitute Adonai or Adon in its place. By this method the scribes (no doubt, in collusion with Rabbis) sought to ensure that the sacred name would not be spoken when the text was read.

The same phenomenon occurs in the Aleppo manuscript, but with a twist. The Aleppo manuscript was written in Tiberias in 930 AD and later transferred to Aleppo, Syria. It was damaged during riots that broke out in Syria after the UN resolution to establish the nation of Israel in 1947. Later, it was smuggled out of Syria and taken to Jerusalem. About 294 out 487 pages survive to date. Some think the Leningrad manuscript was corrected using the Aleppo manuscript.

The sacred name is written in the Aleppo manuscript thousands of times. 4000 or more times the name is missing the middle vowel. However, in a handful of occurrences of the name, all the vowels are included, and they exactly match how the name is written in the Jacob Ben Chayim edition of the Hebrew Old Testament, from which the King James Version was translated. See the examples below.

Fig. 5 [23]

The first example, in Fig. 5, is from Joshua 1:1 and shows two of the places where the middle vowel is missing. Notice there is no silent sheva below the first Hey. According to Hebrew rules, this word is not pronounceable. Even if one tried to pronounce it, all he would get is Yehvah, which still does not match Yahweh. The vowels are not the same. The spelling is different. They are not the same word. Not only that, but, as we will discuss later, the Hebrew letter vav was never generally pronounced like a W, but rather like a V. Today in Israel, the vav is pronounced like a V. Vav is the third letter in the Name of God. So, what we find in these manuscripts does not justify rejecting Jehovah in favor of Yahweh. The spelling is different. They are not the same word. Not only that, but, as we will discuss later, the Hebrew letter vav was never generally pronounced like a W, but rather like a V. Today in Israel, the vav is pronounced like a V. Vav is the third letter in the Name of God. So, what we find in these manuscripts does not justify rejecting Jehovah in favor of Yahweh.

Fig. 6 [24]

Figure 6 above is from 1 Kings 8:11, "So that the priests could not stand to minister because of the cloud: for the glory of the LORD had filled the house of the LORD." The Name is found twice here. The word on the right is the Name without the middle vowel. However, just before that, the scribe wrote the name of God with all the vowels. It appears he forgot to remove the middle vowel and put the full set of vowels in by mistake, or perhaps he did it on purpose. The word reads יְהֹוָה – Yehovah. The two vertical dots above vav are not vowel marks.

Fig. 7 [25]

Figure 7 shows 2 kings 20:9, "And Isaiah said, This sign shalt thou have of the LORD, that the LORD will do the thing that he hath spoken: shall the shadow go forward ten degrees, or go back ten degrees?" YHVH, יהוה, is written twice in this verse. Where it is highlighted, it has the full set of vowels. Once more it is written יְהֹוָה -Yehovah. The O is a single dot above the vav. The full vowels also occur in several other places in the Aleppo manuscript including Ezekiel 3:12, Ezekiel 28:22, and Psalms 26:12. It is only written with the full vowels a few times, but when it has the full vowels, it is written Yehovah. The scribes knew how to write it. YHVH, יהוה, is written twice in this verse. Where it is highlighted, it has the full set of vowels. Once more it is written יְהֹוָה – Yehovah.

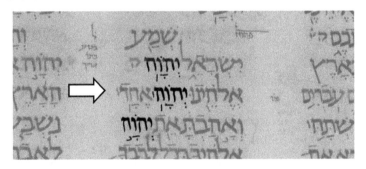

Figure 8 [26]

Figure 8 is from Deuteronomy 6:4,5, "Hear, O Israel: The LORD our God is one LORD: And thou shalt love the LORD thy God with all thine heart, and with all thy soul, and with all thy might." Three times the Sacred Name has the full vowels spelled יְהֹוָה - Yehovah. The fact is that most Hebrew manuscripts with vowel pointing have the name with one vowel missing. However, starting in 2017, Nehemia Gordon and his research team started searching for ancient Hebrew manuscripts that contain the name of Yehovah with the full vowel points. Nehemia is a Karaite Jew, Hebrew scholar, and researcher. His web site is NehemiasWall. As of January 2018, they had found over 1000 manuscripts that have the full name. These manuscripts date from 894 AD onward. The discovery was reported by the Religious News Service on January 25, 2018.

God's name, known as the Tetragrammaton, is written in most Hebrew Bible manuscripts with one of its vowels missing, making it unreadable in accordance with an ancient Jewish ban on speaking the name. Despite this, Gordon had previously discovered five Bible manuscripts with a full set of Hebrew vowels proving the pronunciation of the Tetragrammaton was known to Jewish scribes as "Yehovah."

The project to find new evidence corroborating this discovery, began in February 2017 and in less than one year Gordon found 1,000 more Hebrew Bible manuscripts with the full vowels "Yehovah." These included the two earliest known Hebrew Bible manuscripts with vowels, Russian National Library, Evr. II B 100 from the year 894 AD and the Cairo Codex of the Prophets from 895 AD. Gordon and his team also found the vowels "Yehovah" in three manuscripts written with the lost "Babylonian Pointing," discovered in the Cairo Genizah in 1896. [27]

So, what does all this tell us? It confirms that the Jews have refused to speak the name of God, because it was too holy. It also confirms that the Masoretic scribes made a plan to prevent anyone from reading the Sacred Name. They did this by removing the middle vowel from Yehovah and making it read Yeh?vah. Nevertheless, there were times when the scribes did not remove the middle vowel and wrote the whole name. This revealed the correct way to pronounce the name. The pronunciation was never lost. *One thing you never find in the manuscripts is* יַהְוֶה *Yahweh.*

There is a myth going around the scholarly community that the name Jehovah was invented by a Catholic priest named Galatin or Galantinus in 1520. This myth is several hundred years old. It was apparently started by a gentleman called Drussius, also called Van Der Driesche and Johann Clemens. In his writings published shortly before his death, he expressed the opinion that Galatin had invented Jehovah. Over the years, this opinion has been accepted by scholars as a historical fact. However, this is found to be a true myth. The Aleppo manuscript and the other manuscripts examined by Nehemia Gordon's team (and now, some by you and me) prove that the name Jehovah or Yehovah was known more than 500 years before Galatin could have invented it.

The Witness from Hebrew Names

Hebrew names often contain God's name in a shortened form. A name may start with the first three letters, יהו, and when it does, it is pronounced Yeho. If those same letters end a name, they are pronounced yehu or Yahu, as in Netanyahu, נְתַנְיָהוּ. (Notice the pattern of Netanyahu: CVCVCCVCV. The middle syllable ends with a consonant in the middle of a word. Notice that the final consonant of the syllable in Hebrew has a silent sheva below it, indicating the end of the syllable. Remember our previous discussion at figure 4).

The three letters, יהו, come at the beginning of God's name. If these three letters come at the beginning of names and are pronounced yeho, then when they come at the beginning of God's name, they are pronounced Yeho, not Yahweh. Hebrew is quite consistent about this. Below is a chart showing a few names in the Scriptures, which start with these three letters. Notice how they are pointed. The vowel points are the same as in Yehovah. I suppose the scribes gave *them* the vowel pointing of Adonai also, just to deceive you? Of course not.

Name		English	Reference
יְהוֹשֻׁעַ	Yehoshua	Joshua	Josh. 1:1
יְהוֹיָדָע	Yehoyada	Jehoiada	2 Sam. 8:18
יְהוֹשָׁפָט	Yehoshaphat	Jehoshaphat	1 Kings 22:5
יְהוֹאָשׁ	Yehoash	Jehoash	2 Kings 12:18
יְהוֹאָשׁ	Yeho'ash	Jehoash	2 Kings 12:7
יְהוֹיָכִין	Yehoyachin	Jehoiachin	2 Chron. 36:9
יְהוֹאָחָז	Yeho'achaz	Jehoahaz	2 Kings 13:1
יְהוֹנָדָב	Yehonadav	Jonadab	Jer. 35:14
יְהוֹנָתָן	Yehonathan	Jehonathan	1 Chron 27:25
יְהוֹיָקִים	Yehoyakim	Jehoiakim	2 Kings 23:36
יְהוֹיָרִיב	Yehoyariv	Jehoiarib	1 Chron. 24:7

Fig. 9

Each of these names begin with these letters יְהוֹ which are pronounced Yeho. The Sacred name begins with the exact same letters, which fall under the exact same rules in Hebrew as the other names. Therefore, these letters in God's name are also pronounced Yeho. This, along with the witness of the manuscripts, is incontrovertible proof of how God's sacred name should be pronounced.

The Bible says, *"In the mouth of two or three witnesses shall every word be established"* (2 Corinthians 13:1). We have seen two witnesses to God's name. The manuscripts reveal how the scribes sought to keep the name from being pronounced by removing the middle vowel, O, and we have seen how the scribes left all the vowels in at times revealing how the name is supposed to be pronounced. The second witness is how names are pronounced when they begin with the same three letters that begin God's name. Both the Sacred Name and the other names are pronounced the same. This also confirms that the middle vowel missing in the manuscripts is -O-.

We have seen two witnesses. We are about to see a third.

The Witness of Vav

Vav is the third consonant in the name of God. There are different opinions about how to pronounce vav. In Israel the pronunciation is like an English V. Hebrew scholars and teachers say the ancient pronunciation was like an English W and they call the letter Waw. In the word Yahweh, the w is from vav. If the scholars are wrong, Yahweh is misspelled.

Most scholars agree that the ancient pronunciation of the letter was more like a "W" and less like the "V" that it currently has in the Modern Hebrew language. This assertion has a lot of support if we simply look around at modern use in other Semitic languages. In Arabic, for example, only the "W" sound exists, and the "V" sound does not exist. Among certain Jewish pronunciations, the original still holds true, as Yemenite Jews to this day pronounce the Vav as a "W" in specific cases. When Hebrew is written with pronunciation markings (nikud), a Vav without any markings is pronounced like the "V" in "very," a Vav with a dot in the middle is pronounced "oo," as in "fool," and a Vav with a dot on top is pronounced "o," as in "go." [28]

The Jewish oriented ministry, Time of Reckoning, has a response to this.

> There are scholars who teach that because Hebrew and Arabic are Semitic languages the Hebrew letter ו vav must have been pronounced waw [w] in ancient Hebrew, as it was in Arabic, instead of vav [v]. Although, it is true that both languages are closely related they are not identical and letters from one do not necessarily vocalize the same way in the other. It is also true that vav is vocalized by the Jews in most Arabic-speaking communities as the semivowel [w], i.e. waw; but in some communities of Syria and Egypt, as well as in northwest Morocco, it is vocalized as [v] and in the communities of northeast Morocco the vocalization [w] has the variant [v]. In the Aramaic-speaking communities the same letter is vocalized as [w] while in the Persian-speaking communities the realization is identical to that of soft ב bet, [v]. In all Ashkenazi communities Jews vocalize vav as [v], not waw [w]. Therefore, we can notice that all realizations of vav as waw [w] come from Arabic influence; they are not Hebraic. [29]

Another perspective was expressed by Professor Ben Tziyyon on the web site, Virtual Yeshiva Discussion Forum.

> The earliest Hebrew grammar texts that were produced in a European language were published in Austria and hence were written in German. The Hebrew letter ו (vav) was transliterated by the letter W in those grammar texts because the letter W has the same sound in German as the letter V has in English. Unfortunately, though, the transliteration scheme was overlooked when these grammar books were subsequently

translated into English, and consequently the use of the letter W to represent the Hebrew letter ו (vav) was never corrected to the letter V. From this simple oversight has grown the unshakeable conviction among many Christians that the Hebrew letter ו (vav) "originally" sounded like the English letter W "because books written by Jews say so" and, however many times they are told that this is not the case, they flatly refuse to accept it. [30]

There are several reasons that vav equals V.

Transliteration in European Translations

Reason One is transliteration in European Translations. The Eastern Roman Empire or Byzantine Empire lasted for about one thousand years. In 1453 AD, the Muslim Ottoman Empire conquered the Byzantine Empire and took the capital, Constantinople, later renaming it to Istanbul. The Byzantine empire was a place of great learning. It was the seat of spoken Greek and many Jewish scholars lived there. Many Jews already lived in Europe, but also, when the Byzantine Empire fell, many Jewish scholars fled to western Europe where some of them became teachers. This was a large influence on the Renaissance, which got well underway in the late fifteenth century. So, knowledge of Hebrew was fresh in the early Renaissance and came from the Jews themselves. Even Martin Luther sought out the help of Rabbis when he was translating the Old Testament into German from Hebrew. It was published in 1534.

The Tyndale Bible was first published in 1526 and it transliterated God's name *Iehouah* in Exodus 6. The letter I was pronounced like a Y and U was both pronounced V and later changed to look like V. Therefore, it was pronounced *Yehovah*. The Bishops Bible of 1569 used the same. Later, the Geneva Bible and the King James used the same name. Tyndale translated on the European continent. The translators of the Bishops Bible and the KJV were in England. The translators of the Geneva Bible were in Geneva, Switzerland. The translators of each of these four Bibles had learned that the Hebrew letter vav was to be pronounced as a V.   Therefore, vav was understood to be a V sound as far back as 1526.

Further evidence of this can be seen in how the King James translators translated Hebrew names. The Hebrew name לֵוִי is found in many places in the Old Testament. It is transliterated *Levi*. The letter vav was transliterated as a V. Then, there is the name יָוָן in Genesis 10:2, transliterated Javan. The vav is given a V sound. Then there is the word לִוְיָתָן, Leviathan, in Isaiah 27:1. Again, the vav is transliterated V and given a V sound. Tyndale also did the same in Genesis 10:2 and 29:34, in 1526.   The same thing occurs in Martin Luther's German translation of the Old Testament, published in 1534. In Genesis 10:2, Martin Luther wrote *Javan*. In Genesis 29:34, Martin Luther wrote *Levi* and in Isaiah 27:1, he wrote *Leviathan*. All of this confirms that the understanding of translators in the sixteenth and seventeenth centuries was that vav was pronounced with a V sound (and they learned Hebrew from teachers who lived in the fifteenth century).

The amazing thing is that the Hebrew scholars responsible for the NASV and the LSB, *know this*! When you examine Genesis 10:2, Genesis 29:34, and Isaiah 27:1 in the LSB, you find an incredible thing. You *do not* find Jawan, Lewi, and Lewiathan. No, it is not written like that. When the LSB translators encountered the Hebrew vav in those names, they transliterated the vav as a V! They wrote Javan in Genesis 10, Levi in Genesis 29, and Leviathan in Isaiah 27. But, in God's name, they made the vav a W and wrote Yahweh. This is inconsistent and dishonest. There is absolutely no excuse for this kind of inconsistency.

The Hebrew Language

Hebrew is the second reason. There are two letters in Hebrew that sound like V. Bet is the second letter in the Hebrew alphabet. It has two forms and two sounds and two names. Bet בּ has a dot inside it and sounds like an English B. Vet or soft Bet ב has no dot and sounds like an English V. The other letter is the third letter in God's name, vav ו.

There is a word in Hebrew that can be spelled two different ways. Each way it is spelled, it means the same and is pronounced the same. The word is גֵו, gav, spelled gimel vav. It means *back*, as in the back of a human. It can be found in eight places in the Old Testament.

One of those times was Prov. 10:13, "a rod *is* for the back of him that is void of understanding." The same word is given a variant spelling in Ezekiel 43:13, "and this shall be the higher place of the altar." The word translated *higher place* in this verse is גַּב, gimel vet, and it also means *back*. גַּב means more than *back*. That is why it translated "higher place" in Exek. 43:13. However, it does mean *back* and is so translated in Ps 129:3 and Ezek. 10:12, according to Strong's Hebrew Dictionary. [31] Therefore, it is a synonym of גַו, gav. It is also translated *back* in Daniel 7:6 in the Aramaic section of Daniel 1-7. It is usually marked as Aramaic at this place, but it is a Hebrew word. Apparently, it is a Hebrew loan word to Aramaic.

The point of all this is that we have two words which are synonyms and are spelled different. The fact that one is spelled with a vav and the other with a vet, gives us a clue as to how vav is pronounced. Vet ב is definitely pronounced as a V. This indicates that vav was also pronounced as a V in ancient Hebrew.

There are other similar examples from ancient Hebrew. The following example comes from the Mishnah, which is the collection of oral traditions or oral Torah embodying the authoritative interpretations of the Torah. Nehemia Gordon says this about this example.

> Another later proof that vet and *vav* were interchangeable to ancient Hebrew speakers is found in the Mishnah (AD 200) relating to the spelling of the town of Yavneh. The v in *Yavneh* is sometimes spelled with a *vav* and sometimes with a *vet*. These spelling variants are found in the *Mishnah* RH 4:2 (Kaufmann MS. A50 76v) and *Avot* 4:4 (Kaufmann MS. A50 171v). Another example of the interchangeable vav-vet is found in the same MS where the word geese is sometimes spelled with both letters (Shabbat 24:3 and Hullin 12:2). [32]

Nehemia Gordon also gave an example from a Jewish poet who wrote in the sixth century.

> Further proof that the ancient Jews pronounced vav with a v and not a w are found in some Jewish poetry from the 6th century AD by Elazar Kalir and Yanai Israel.

For example, Kalir (who lived in Tiberias, Israel) rhymes (via alliteration or the repeating of consonantal sounds) the words *Levi* and *navi*. Levi he spells with a *vav* and *navi* he spells with a vet. What makes this poem so compelling is that he uses words containing the letter vet eight times, and the ninth time he uses a *vav* in place of a vet (in the word Levi). The rhyming in this poem would make no sense at all to have nine v sounds and then a w sound if *vav* were pronounced as a w instead of a v (MS Oxford, Bodleian 2714, fol52a) This poem is actually based on Jer 23:8–9, which prophesies the ingathering of the exiles. Similarly, Yanai in one of his poems rhymes *y'chaveh* (tell) with *ye'aveh* (swell). The former word is spelled with a *vav*, while the latter word is spelled with a vet (MS Cambridge University, Taylor-Schecter H17–4). [33]

All of this, along with the understanding of the translators long ago, gives strong evidence that the original sound of the vav is V not W. *That means Yahweh cannot be the right name of the creator, because it is misspelled!*

Yahweh, a Horrifying Connection

It was not until the eighteenth and nineteenth centuries that Yahweh became popular among Hebrew Scholars, most of whom were Gentiles. At first it was promoted by liberal scholars. Now evangelical scholars have embraced it to the point that John MacArthur approves its use in the Legacy Standard Bible. Where did it originate? The LSB Preface gives this answer.

> The translation "Yahweh" is substantiated by scholarly reconstruction as well as by historical discussions in Theodoret, Epiphanius, Clement of Alexandria, Origen, and Aquila. Consequently, those latter individuals affirm the usage of God's covenant name in the period of the early church. Preserving this in translation foundationally records what is present in the OT text. [34]

Several names are mentioned in this quote: Theodoret, Epiphanius, Clement, Origen, and Aquila. Who are they? Theodoret was a bishop and theologian of the school of Antioch. He lived from 393 to 458 AD. Epiphanius was a Christian bishop who lived from 310 to 403. Clement was the head and a teacher at the so-called Christian school of Alexandria, Egypt, a school that mixed Greek philosophy with Christianity. He lived from 150 to 215 AD. Aquila of Sinope was a second century Jewish scholar who translated the Old Testament from Hebrew into Greek. Only a few fragments of this work remain. Finally, Origen was a scholar and theologian of Alexandria, who also taught in the school there. He lived from 184 to 254 AD. Some think he was one of the greatest Christian scholars who ever lived and, others think he was the one of the greatest heretics. Bear in mind, all examples of God's name from these men come from Greek, not Hebrew.

A web article entitled *Yahweh, Jupiter of the Hosts (18th Century A.D.)*, lists the name of God given in Greek by several ancient sources from the twelfth century BC to the fifth century AD. In most cases, the name is Ιαω, pronounced in English as Yao. Clement and Origen used that name. Epiphanius and Theodoret used that name, but they also used the name Ιαβε, pronounced Yave (the β, beta, has a V sound), or it can be transliterated Yahveh. This last name is the most significant historically. The above article says this about Epiphanius and Theodoret.

> The debate between the names of Yahweh and Jehovah came to a climax in A.D. 1707, when the German Orientalist Adrian Relaand reprinted the views of several scholars, saying Yahweh was more likely. Jehovah was considered to be an invention of the Middle Ages, but Yahweh could be seen in the writings of Epiphanius and Theodoret.

But Where Did It Come From?

> Epiphanius (c. A.D. 375) told us that the name Ιαβε was used by certain Gnostics. The Gnostics were famous for combining the stories of Greek and Roman gods with Christianity.

Ιαβε was used by the Bishop Theodoret of Cyrus (c. A.D. 450). But he seems to have just gotten this pronunciation from Epiphanius' book *Against Heresies*. Later, Theodoret used Iabai as the pronunciation of YHVH. [35]

Ιαβαι (Iabai and same meaning and pronunciation as Ιαβε) can also be transliterated Yahveh, according to its sounds.

Later in history, another player entered the story. Wilhelm Gesenius (1786-1842) was a German Lutheran theologian, Biblical scholar, Biblical critic, and linguist in Halle, Germany. He has been credited with making the name Yahweh popular. He published a large Hebrew and Chaldee (Aramaic) lexicon in 1829. In it, he wrote a significant article on the name of God. In part, that article said the following with this author's comments in brackets.

> Others, as Reland (decad. exercitatt. de vera pronunciatione nominis Jehova, Traj. ad Rh. 1707, 8.), **following the Samaritans**, suppose that יַהְוֶה [Yahveh or Yahweh] was anciently the true pronunciation, and they have an additional ground for the opinion in the abbreviated forms יָהוּ [yahu] and יָה [Yah]. Also those who consider that יְהֹוָה [Yehovah] was the actual pronunciation (Michaelis in Supplem. p. 524), are not altogether without ground on which to defend their opinion. In this way can the abbreviated syllables יְהוֹ [Yeho] and יוֹ [Yo], with which many proper names begin, be more satisfactorily explained. [36] (author's emphasis)

"Reland" no doubt means Adriaan Reland (1676-1818) a noted Dutch orientalist who achieved fluency in Arabic, Hebrew, and other Semitic languages. It is remarkable that Gesenius says Reland followed *the Samaritans* in the pronunciation of, יהוה, the name of God. It is clearly stated that the Samaritans pronounced the name of God as Yahweh. Theodoret also said the Samaritan used Yahweh or Ιαβε in Greek.

Is that significant?

The Samaritan's are a people living in Israel and elsewhere in the world, who are descended from both Israelites and gentiles. In 722 BC, Assyrian armies swept into the northern tribes of Israel and conquered their capital, Samaria. According to 2 Kings 17, the King of Assyria took the Israelite people captive and removed them from the land to Halah and Habor and the cities of the Medes. He then brought gentile people from other lands and placed them in the cities of Israel, which was also called Samaria. Lions began to attack the new inhabitants and they concluded it was because they did not know the way of the "God of the land." So, the King of Assyria sent them an Israelite priest to teach them. The result was not good.

> 32 So they feared the LORD, and made unto themselves of the lowest of them priests of the high places, which sacrificed for them in the houses of the high places.
> 33 They feared the LORD, and served their own gods, after the manner of the nations whom they carried away from thence.
> 34 Unto this day they do after the former manners: they fear not the LORD, neither do they after their statutes, or after their ordinances, or after the law and commandment which the LORD commanded the children of Jacob, whom he named Israel (2 Kings 17:32-34)

Even is Jesus' day, the Samaritans had an imperfect worship. When Jesus spoke with the Samaritan woman in John 4, she said to Him:

> 20 Our fathers worshipped in this mountain; and ye say, that in Jerusalem is the place where men ought to worship.
> 21 Jesus saith unto her, Woman, believe me, the hour cometh, when ye shall neither in this mountain, nor yet at Jerusalem, worship the Father.
> 22 **Ye worship ye know not what:** we know what we worship: for salvation is of the Jews. (John 4:20-22)

The mountain the Samaritan woman was referring to was Mount Gerizim. The Samaritans had built a temple there about the time the Jews were restoring the temple and walls of Jerusalem beginning in 536 BC (see the books of Ezra and Nehemiah). About 109 BC, the Samaritan temple was destroyed by a Jewish priest, John Hyrcanus. The ruins of that temple can be found there today.

Alexander the Great (356-323 BC) conquered the Persian empire and built an empire of his own. After Alexander died, his successors divided the empire into four parts. Two of Alexander's generals were significant for the following history of Israel and the Samaritans. Ptolemy took Egypt founding the Ptolemaic Empire and Seleucus Nicator took Syria, Mesopotamia, and Central Asia, founding the Seleucid Empire. Until the Romans gained control of Syria and Egypt and Israel between them, the Seleucid Empire and Egypt fought for control of Israel. Several times, control of Israel passed from one to the other.

In 175 BC, Antiochus IV Epiphanes ascended the throne of the Seleucid Empire. He was a vicious persecutor of the Jews. In 168 BC, Antiochus led a second, but unsuccessful, campaign against Egypt. On his return trip to Syria, he paused through Judea, a land where the Seleucid Empire held power. While there, he committed great atrocities. He killed and tortured many of the Jewish people, he looted the treasures of the temple in Jerusalem, he sacrificed pigs on the altar of the temple in Jerusalem and on other altars he had built around the country, compelled the Jews to forsake the worship of God, and many other persecutions.

Hearing of these things and knowing that Antiochus was coming their way, the Samaritans decided to become proactive. According to Flavius Josephus (37-100 AD), the first century Jewish Historian, they made some decisions and sent a letter to Antiochus. This is what it said.

> To king Antiochus the god, Epiphanes, a memorial from the Sidonians, who live at Shechem. Our forefathers, upon certain frequent plagues, and as following a certain ancient superstition, had a custom of observing that day which by the Jews is called the Sabbath. And when they had erected a temple at the mountain called Gerrizzim, though without a name, they offered upon it the proper sacrifices. Now, upon the just

treatment of these wicked Jews, those that manage their affairs, supposing that we were of kin to them, and practiced as they do, make us liable to the same accusations, although we be originally Sidonians, as is evident from the public records. We therefore beseech thee, our benefactor and Savior, to give order to Apollonius, the governor of this part of the country, and to Nicanor, the procurator of thy affairs, to give us no disturbance, nor to lay to our charge what the Jews are accused for, since we are aliens from their nation, and from their customs; **but let our temple, which at present hath no name at all be named the Temple of Jupiter Hellenius.** If this were once done, we should be no longer disturbed, but should be more intent on our own occupation with quietness, and so bring in a greater revenue to thee. [37] (Emphasis the Author's)

Previously, the Samaritan temple had no name, but at that time they requested the temple be named "The Temple of Jupiter Hellenius" (*Hellenius* referred to Greece). By this, they hoped to avoid the fate of the Jews. Antiochus granted them the request and they escaped the persecution he had heaped upon the Jews. However, an apostate people had now committed themselves to paganism.

Jupiter was the king of the gods of the Romans, the god of the sky and lightening. He was also called *Jove*. In Latin, Jupiter is spelled *Iuppiter* and Jove is spelled *Iove*. The name Iuppiter is a combination of *Iovis* (the genitive form of Iove) and *Pater*. Together they mean *Father Jove*. So, the word Jupiter means Father Jove. Jove (or Iove in Latin) is this god's name. In classical Latin, the I in *Iove* is pronounced like y in *yes*; the o is like o in *off*; and the v is pronounced like a w. *That makes the English transliteration of Iove to be* **Yahweh**.

The W sound does not exist in Greek. Therefore, *Iove* in Greek is Ιαβε, which is transliterated *Yahveh*. Does this Greek name look familiar? It should. It is the word Epiphanius and Theodoret used for the name of God almighty.

Let's put the facts together.

1.   Epiphanius and Theodoret said the name of God is Ιαβε, Yahveh. Where did this name come from? Did it come from Hebrew? No, it did not.

2.   Gensenius said Reland was following the Samaritans in the use of this name. theodoret also said it came from the Samaritans. The Samaritans, not the jews, used it before Theodoret or Epiphanius. Did the Samaritans get the name from Hebrew or some other source?

3.   In 168 BC, the Samaritans named their temple "The Temple of Jupiter Hellenius." They embraced the name of Jupiter, the King of the gods.

4.   Jupiter's name in Latin is Iove, pronounced Yahweh.

5.   Jupiter's name in Greek is Ιαβε, pronounced Yahveh. This is the very name embraced by Epiphanius and Theodoret, following the example of the Samaritans.

This connection implies some very scary things. First, it implies that the word Yahweh does not come from Hebrew, but rather from Latin and Greek. Second, this Latin and Greek name is the name of Jupiter. Finally, it is not the name of God, but, in the final analysis, it is the name of a pagan god.

If this connection is correct, and I think it is, **the LSB has replaced God's name in the Old Testament with the name of a pagan god!**

The LSB Old Testament Disconnect

Is Jesus God or is He *A* god? When one studies the King James Bible, there is no question that Jesus is God. One simple verse settles that question. "**God** was manifest in the flesh... (1 Tim. 3:16). But, the LSB obscures that verse. "**He who** was manifested in the flesh ..." (1 Tim. 3:16 LSB). However, the problem is worse than that in the LSB.

John MacArthur and the LSB translators decided to change the centuries old practice of translating the Hebrew name of God, Jehovah, as LORD. They chose to transliterate the name by using Yahweh. However, Jehovah is the only name they transliterated (albeit incorrectly). None of the other references to God were transliterated, such as Elohim (God), El (God), El-shaddai (God Almighty), and Adonai

(Lord). All of these were translated with the English words God or Lord. Also, they do not use Yahweh any place God's name is found in the New Testament. In Matthew 3:3 there is an exact quote from Isaiah 40:3 in the KJB, although the LSB changed it slightly. "Prepare the way for Yahweh ..." (Is. 40:3 LSB) "Make ready the way of the LORD ..." (Mat. 3:3 LSB). In Isaiah 40:3 the word is Yahweh. But, in Matthew 3:3 they used LORD instead. That doesn't seem very consistent. The real problem is worse than that.

The KJB does it differently, of course. Most of the time the sacred name of God is used in the Old Testament, the KJB translates it LORD with capital letters. In the New Testament, Jesus is consistently called the Lord: "no man can say that Jesus is the Lord, but by the Holy Ghost" (1 Cor. 12:3). This automatically connects Him to the LORD of the Old Testament.

In the LSB, that connection is lost. The LSB Old Testament calls God Yahweh and the LSB New Testament calls Jesus Lord (not capital letters). In the LSB, 1 Corinthians 12:3 says, 'no one can say, "Jesus is Lord," except by the Holy Spirit.' In Matthew 3:2 in the LSB, the word LORD is spelled with all capitals indicating it is the sacred name. However, Jesus is called Lord, but not in all capitals. This clearly disconnects Jesus with the God of the Old Testament. This disconnect is exacerbated, perhaps explained, in John 1, when Jesus is called "the only begotten God" (John 1:18). In the LSB, Jesus is not the God of the Old Testament. He is a lesser god begotten by the God of the Old Testament. Not only is this Gnosticism, but *this is the exact doctrinal position of the heretical cult who say they are Jehovah's witnesses and are not.*

Chapter Three
How Should God's Name be Translated

The LSB chose to transliterate the name of God given in Exodus 6 from Hebrew letters into English letters. In doing so, they chose the wrong name Yahweh instead of Jehovah. However, when they translated Greek into English they used LORD, not Yahweh. I consider this to be inconsistent at the least.

How should a translator handle the name of God? Taking that name from Hebrew into English is one thing, but what about French, German, Swahili, Busuku, Kinyarwanda, Kikuyu, or another of the over 7000 languages on earth? Let's begin by looking at how God Translated His name.

How God Translated His Name

It seems that, when a discussion of ancient manuscripts, scribal methods, and so forth take place, the little matter of inspiration gets forgotten. People talk about manuscripts, scholarly opinions, and the style and word choices of New Testament writers as if they are the final authority. Similarly, the LSB appealed to the authority of ancient writers in choosing to use the word Yahweh. God seems to get lost in the discussion. It seems to be forgotten that the words of the New Testament are the words of God, the words God chose. In this discussion we will not forget. The New Testament was inspired in Greek and for a few minutes we will appeal to the Greek New Testament.

There are many quotes in the New Testament that come from the Old Testament. Some of these quotes are paraphrases. They are like the way some of us preach, saying, "The Bible says ... ," then we paraphrase what the Bible teaches. Other quotes are partially paraphrased and partially exact quotes. Others are nearly exact quotes. These quotes sometimes contain the sacred name of God, taken from Hebrew, Jehovah, and put in Greek. Both the Hebrew Old Testament and the Greek New Testament were inspired by God. Obviously, they are two different languages. When someone takes a word in Hebrew and puts it into Greek, it is an act of *translation*, regardless of who did it. So, when God took words He inspired in Hebrew and put them into Greek, He also was translating. How, then, did God translate His Holy name from Hebrew onto Greek? Let's look at both Hebrew names Elohim and Jehovah.

In Hebrew, Elohim is a plural noun that means God. It is used in Genesis 1:1 and many times afterwards. Look at the following examples of Old Testament quotes in the New Testament.

>   1)   Ezek. 37:27 with 2 Cor. 6:16
>   Ezek. 37:27 - I will be their **God** (עֲלֵיהֶם Elohim), and they shall be my people.
>   2 Cor. 6:16 - ... I will be their **God** (θεός Theos)
>   2)   Ps 45:6 with Hebrews 1:8
>   Ps. 45:6 – Thy throne, O **God** (אֱלֹהִים Elohim), is for ever and ever
>   Hebrews 1:8 - Thy throne, O **God** (θεός Theos), is for ever and ever

When God translated Elohim into Greek in the New Testament, He chose to use the Greek word *theos*. *Theos* is explained in Acts 17:23 where Paul told the philosophers on Mars Hill, "For as I passed by, and beheld your devotions, I found an altar with this inscription, TO THE UNKNOWN GOD" (θεός theos). From this, we learn that theos was a general or generic religious term the Greeks used to designate a god, just like the English word god is a general word for deity and can apply to the true God or to a pagan god.   Secondly, we also learn that theos was a name applied to pagan gods and no wonder, because the Greeks were pagans. Nevertheless, rather than transliterate the Hebrew name into Greek letters, or make a new name altogether, God chose the pagan Greek name θεός, the name of the "unknown theos," when He inspired the New Testament.

We have already discussed God's name, Jehovah. Below are three examples of how God translated His name into Greek.

>   1)   Isaiah 40:3 with Matthew 3:3
>   Isaiah 40:3 - Prepare ye the way of the LORD (יְהֹוָה Jehovah)
>   Matthew 3:3 - Prepare ye the way of the Lord (Κυρίος Lord)
>   2)   Deuteronomy 6:16 with Matthew 4:7

Deuteronomy 6:16 - Ye shall not tempt the LORD (יְהֹוָה Jehovah) your God

Matthew 4:7 - Thou shalt not tempt the Lord (Κυρίος Kurios) thy God

3)   Ps. 118:26 with Luke 19:38

Psalms 118:26 - Blessed be he that cometh in the name of the LORD: (יְהֹוָה – Jehovah)

Luke 19:38 - Blessed be the King that cometh in the name of the Lord (κύριος Kurios– Lord)

Here are three examples showing how God chose to translate His own Hebrew name, Jehovah. How could it be any clearer? God did not inspire the New Testament writers to write Jehovah and He certainly did not inspire them to write Yahweh. He did not inspire them to write Elohim, either. He inspired them to use the Greek name Theos for Elohim and He inspired them to use Kurios for Yehovah. Not only that, but when he wanted the world to know that His Son has a *name that is above every name*, He inspired them to write the Greek name Iesous (Ἰησοῦς), or Jesus. Jesus' Hebrew name is Yeshuah, which means Jehovah saves. However, God did not inspire the New Testament writers to use the name Yeshuah. He inspired the Greek name Jesus, which also means *Jehovah saves*!

How Should We Translate His Name?

We've seen how God handled translating His name from Hebrew to Greek. Can we learn anything from this about how to translate from Hebrew or Greek into other languages? I think it teaches us exactly how to do it. Since God translated Jehovah into Kurios and God into Theos, let us first understand a little more about Theos and Kurios.

Theos was not just a generic word for God, it also referred to a specific god that the Athenians worshipped. His nature and name were unknown to them. They called this god, the unknown god (Acts 17:23). The word theos was a generic name for a god in general. Zeus was a theos, Ares was a theos, Apollo was a theos, etc. The generic nature of the word and the unknown aspect of the "unknown god" made theos the perfect name to represent the God of the Bible. Before Paul's time the Greeks had been prepared for this. Three Greek philosophers, Xenophanes, Plato, and Aristotle had used the term *Theos* as a personal name for *one Supreme God* in their writings. So, God led the Apostles to appropriate the word as the personal name of the Supreme Creator God of the Scriptures. [38]

Kurios means several things. It is clearly used to refer to Jehovah of the Old Testament (Mt. 1:20, 21) and it refers to the Lord Jesus Christ (Acts 16:31). However, it also refers to people in different ways. It is the title of the owner of a vineyard (Mt. 20:8), of the master of a house (Mk 13:35), of a master of servants (Mt. 24:45-46; Eph. 6:5), and of husbands (1 Peter 3:6). It is used for the title *sir* and applied to masters (Mt. 13:27; Jn 4:11, 15), fathers (Mt. 21:30), the Roman Procurator (Mt 27:63), and as an address of respect (Jn 12:21; Jn 20:15; Act 16:30). Kurios is used in similar ways in Standard Modern Greek and is also used for the direct address, mister. So, the word Kurios means Lord (God), lord (a ruler), master, and sir. In other words, kurios is a word that speaks of one who is in authority.

Seeing that these are the meanings of theos and Kurios, how do we go about deciding on a name for God in other languages? God declared His name to be Yehovah in Hebrew and, as God, He is called Elohim in Hebrew. However, when He inspired His Word in Greek to reach those who speak and read Greek, he chose to call Himself by Greek names, Theos and Kurios. Does He have names in the other languages of the world?

Principle 1: Choose a Name from the Native Culture

God has revealed himself to all nations. Remember, after the waters of the great Flood receded and the earth dried, only Noah and his three sons and their wives were still alive out of all the billions (probably) on earth. They began to multiply right away. Instead of scattering to refill the earth, they began to migrate to find a new home. By the time their migration had brought them to the valley of Shinar (Genesis 11), they had grown into a large number. At that time, they all knew a number of things about God.

1) They knew God is the supreme being.
2) They knew God is the creator of all things.
3) They knew what sin is.

4)   They knew God demanded righteousness.
5)   They knew God judged the entire world for sin in a great world-wide flood.

Up to that time they had always had one language. When God divided their one language into many, surely, He did not leave His name to only one language. Without doubt, He gave each group His name in their language.

After God divided their single language into many and disbursed each nation/language group, they still had the knowledge of God strongly in their hearts. They had enough knowledge to believe in Him and worship Him. God "hath made of one blood all nations of men for to dwell on all the face of the earth, and hath determined the times before appointed, and the bounds of their habitation; That they should seek the Lord, if haply they might feel after him, and find him, though he be not far from every one of us" (Acts 17:26-27). If God wanted each new ethnic language group to continue worshipping Him, then *surely He planted in each language the name by which He wanted to be known, so they could worship Him by name.* He did not want all nations to know Hebrew, but He wants the entire world to know His name (Ps. 148:11-14). After Babel (Gen. 11), God led each migrating nation to a land where they could live separately from other nations. They still had all the knowledge they needed to know and worship Him, including His name in their language. All these nations began as monotheistic, and only later did many of them sink into idolatry. Still, many others remained monotheistic. Not all have completely forgotten what they learned in the days of the flood and following. God describes it this way.

> For the wrath of God is revealed from heaven against all ungodliness and unrighteousness of men, who hold the truth in unrighteousness; Because that which may be known of God is manifest in them; for God hath shewed it unto them. For the invisible things of him from the creation of the world are clearly seen, being understood by the things that are made, even his eternal power and Godhead; so that they are without excuse: Because that, when they knew God, they glorified him not as God, neither were thankful; but

became vain in their imaginations, and their foolish heart was darkened. Professing themselves to be wise, they became fools, And changed the glory of the uncorruptible God into an image made like to corruptible man, and to birds, and fourfooted beasts, and creeping things. (Rom. 1:18-23)

These verses reveal the existence of general revelation. Not all revelation is restricted to the Bible. Some of it comes from God's creation. This revelation goes out to all nations without exception (Ps. 19:1-6; Rom. 10:18). The nations not only had knowledge of God from God's works in the pre-flood world, but they were reminded of much of that information from the world around them. From the creation, the nations learn the existence of an invisible creator who is eternal and all powerful. They learn enough that they can know of Him, find Him, glorify Him, and be thankful. God has not left Himself without a witness among the many peoples of the world. "Nevertheless he left not himself without witness, in that he did good, and gave us rain from heaven, and fruitful seasons, filling our hearts with food and gladness" (Acts 14:17). It seems reasonable to believe that God has also revealed His name in each of the many languages of the world.

In addition to the information about God they learn from creation, the nations have the witness of their conscience.

> 14 For when the Gentiles, which have not the law, do **by nature** the things contained in the law, these, having not the law, are a law unto themselves: 15 Which shew the **work of the law written in their hearts, their conscience also bearing witness,** and their thoughts the mean while accusing or else excusing one another;) (Rom. 2:14-15)

Though the nations have sank into sin and error, many retain enough knowledge that they can still connect with the gospel when they hear it, including the name God gave them. *One of the ways missionaries can decide what name to use when translating the name of God into various languages is to follow the example of Paul.* As we have seen, he took a pagan name of god and, under the leading of the Holy Spirit, adopted that name to be the name of God and added teaching that refined the name to make it mean all the Bible teaches about God. The peoples of the world use various names to describe their gods. Many of these peoples have a name for a true supreme creator God who created all things. In many cases, their belief in this name is pure enough to allow it to be adopted as the name of the God of the Bible. Any misunderstandings the people have about this god can be corrected through Bible translation and teaching. Next, we will see some examples of the adoption of the name.

The Santal

In 1867 two missionaries, Lars Skrefsrud and Hans Borreson, found a people north of Calcutta, India called the **Santal.** They learned that the Santal believed in a deity called **Thakur Jiu** (which means "genuine god"). After hearing the missionary messages, Santal sages insisted that Thakur Jiu was the right name for God. To the Santal this God represented the supreme God that their people worshipped in ancient times. However, they no longer worshipped Him at the time the missionaries came. They had served Thakur Jiu at first, but later turned to spiritism and became captive to the worship of demons. As they studied the history of the beliefs of the people, the missionaries found that "Thakur Jiu" did not have any disqualifying beliefs attached to Him. They found Thakur Jiu to be in the "theos" category. Their acceptance of this name had a great and positive effect on the Santal people. It led to great interest and widespread conversions. [39]

The Gedeo

Several million people in tribes of south-central Ethiopia have a common belief in **Mangano,** the benevolent creator of all that is. One of these tribes is called the **Gedeo** Tribe. Few of them actually worshipped Mangano. They were more concerned about appeasing an evil being named Sheit'an. They did this because they felt so separated from Mangano that they could not renounce Sheit'an. In 1948, missionaries, Albert Brant and Glen Cain, came among the Gedeo. They found there several who claimed to have been told of their coming in visions from Mangano. They also found Mangano to be in the same category as Thakur Jiu. There was a great response of the Gedeo to the Gospel. Many were thankful for the opportunity to be reconciled to

Mangano through Jesus Christ. Three decades later there were more than 200 churches among the Gedeo averaging more than 200 members each. [40]

The Mbaka

A similar story can be told about the **Mbaka** of the Central African Republic. The designation of the creator in several Bantu languages is *Koro*. Many of the Mbaka were already prepared to respond to the gospel when Ferdinand Rosenau and his Baptist colleagues preached to them in the early 1920's. The Mbaka not only believed that Koro was the supreme creator God, but they also believed that Koro had sent His Son to do "something" wonderful for mankind. They were resolved that whenever Koro's messengers arrived, they would listen and believe their message. Koro was a logical choice of a word for God. [41]

Swahili

The **Swahili** language is one of two official languages of the seven countries of the East African Community and is a common trade language of others. The name for God in Swahili is **Mungu**. It is a derivative of the ancient name of the creator God **Mulungu**, which is used in the Yao, Nyamwezi, Shambaa, Kamba, Sukuma, Rufiji, and Turu languages. Mulungu or Mungu was known as the great creator god and became the names of the God of the Bible in these languages and in Swahili. [42]

The Kikuyu

The **Kikuyu** people of Kenya worshipped **Ngai**, along with the Embu, Meru, and Kamba groups of Kenya, and the Maasai of Kenya and Tanzania. Ngai was the omnipotent creator of the universe and everything in it. Ngai is now the God of the Bible and worshipped by believers among these people groups. [43]

The Bukusu

The **Bukusu** people of Kenya are one of the twenty tribes of the Luhya Bantu people, and they speak a language called Busuku. In pre-Christian days, they believed **Wele** is the creator of all (Wele Khaumbi). After he created, he divided all things (Wele khakaba). In their tradition.

Wele created the first man (Mwambu, the inventor) out of *mud* at a place called Mumbo, which means "west." In the Genesis account, God created man from *dust* and drove man out of the garden of Eden toward the east (Gen. 3:34). So, when Adam looked back at the garden, he was looking *west*. [44]

The Luo

There is in Kenya and Tanzania near Lake Victoria a people known as the **Luo**. They are the fourth largest tribe in Kenya and speak a language known as Dholuo. The traditional name of their God is **Nyasaye**. The Luo belief about Nyasaye is described in the following way.

> The Luo recognize a supreme being whose common name is Nyasaye. He is described as Nyakalaga, the one who dwells everywhere. Legend attributes to Nyasaye an anthropomorphic form. He works and continues to support the universe he created in the totality of his creation. Nyasaye is considered to be without matter. He is powerful and intervenes directly in the daily activities of man. He can create and destroy man. He can send various sicknesses, disasters, and punishment when he is angry. He is also the source of man's blessing (gueth). [45]

All of these and many other people groups have a traditional name for a god who is considered the supreme being of the universe and the creator. In many cases, missionaries have determined that this god is in the same category as Theos was among the Greek speaking people of the first century and, therefore, the traditional name qualifies as the name of the Lord God in their languages.

Kurios:

There is great similarity in how Kurios is used in Greek and the uses of the English word *Lord*. In Modern American usage, *Lord* is limited to Deity for the most part, but not in British and early American usage. *Lord* was used for a ruler, a governor, a husband, a father, a nobleman, and the owner of a house (e.g., lord of the manor). [46] In these things, the English word *lord* is a good match to Kurios and, therefore, to Jehovah.

The conclusion is simple. Since God chose Kurios in Greek to equal Jehovah in Hebrew and the definitions and usage of Kurios reasonably match the English word *Lord, then the English Lord is the proper and correct translation of the Hebrew name Jehovah.* Lord is also the right word to translate kurios when it refers to Jesus Christ.

Is this true in other languages also? When I was in Germany, I went several times to a German Christian youth center. There was an older man there several times, who would walk by me and say, "Preis den Herr" (praise the Lord). The German word for the Lord was *Herr.* However, the word Herr means more than that. It also means sir, mister, gentleman, master, and ruler. It is a very good match to Kurios.

Other European languages follow the same pattern. The **Spanish** words for "the Lord" are "El Señor." Señor also means other things, similar to what Herr means. In **Swedish**, *herre* means gentleman, lord, sir, master, mister, Sir, and (when capitalized) the Lord. In **Slovene**, *Gospod* means Lord, sir, mister, and gentleman. The **Portuguese** *Senhor* means Lord, master, sir, mister, and gentleman. Romanian has *domnul*, which means Lord, mister, and gentleman. The word *Kungs* in **Latvian** has a similar range of meanings as does the **Italian** word *Signore,* Lord, lord, master, gentleman, and mister. The **Icelandic** term *drottinn* means lord, king, Lord, god, master. The **Dutch** word *Heer* means Lord, mister, and gentleman. In **Danish**, the word Herre is used to mean Lord, master, mister, gentleman, and sir. Some of the same meanings accompany the word *Gospodina* in **Croation,** such as lord, mister, and gentleman. In **Hungarian**, it is Úr, meaning lord and gentleman.

All these European languages have a word that is clearly a match for Kurios. For some of them this is no wonder because of the influence of Greek and Latin and how some of them influenced each other. Nevertheless, there are languages in Africa that are similar without the influence of Latin and Greek. In **Swahili**, the word ***Bwana*** is used for the Lord. It also means sir. The **Kikuyu** of Kenya say ***Mwathani***, which means Lord, master, ruler. The **Luo** tribe of Kenya and Tanzania use the word ***Ruoth***, meaning lord and king. When it applies to Jehovah and Jesus Christ, the translation of the term *Kurios* requires a word that speaks of authority, rulership, power and is a term commanding respect.

Principle 2: Contextual Conditioning

In spite of the provision God may have made for a group to know and understand Him, there may be people groups where God's name has been lost or corrupted beyond the ability of a missionary to use it. They may have names for gods and spirits, and all of them may be irreparably filled with meaning that is more closely associated with demons rather than God. What is the missionary to do then? How does he translate the name of God is a situation in which there is no pre-existing name for God? The answer is *contextual conditioning*.

Contextual conditioning is based on helping people learn new meanings for words. This is done by a combination of teaching and reading the word in the Scriptures. Teaching is important even if the language has a good word for God and the Lord. But, teaching is especially important if a missionary has to give a meaning to a word that is different than its current meaning in the general culture. It is also necessary to translate the Bible to give the people the opportunity to read the new word in the Scriptures.

There are a certain ways to choose a word that the missionary can condition in its cultural context. *The first is to choose a word from another language.* Every language has loan words from other languages. English has picked up words from German, Spanish, Greek, Latin, French, and so on. Other languages have adopted words from English. The English word *God* originally came from another language, probably from old Germanic and some trace it back to Sanskrit. As seen in the examples above, several languages in Africa share a name for God. One example is Ngai, who is worshipped by the Kikuyu, Embu, Meru, and Kamba groups of Kenya, all of whom speak diverse mother tongues. A name may possibly be chosen from a neighboring group barring any prejudice or enmity between the groups.

Another possibility is to coin a word for God. One example involves the Yagaria of Papua, New Guinea. Dr. Charles Turner, former Director of the Baptist Bible Translator's Institute, explained it this way.

> In the Yagaria language of Papua, New Guinea, the word *God* was transliterated as "Got." Yagaria phonemic structure does not allow this word to end in a

consonant, so an "l" was added, and the name for God became *Goti*.

Naturally, this word did not mean much the first time the Yagaria people heard it. Through the translation of the New Testament and many years of teaching, the word *Goti* has come to mean the God of the Bible.

The word *Goti* became the nearest formal equivalent of the word God by contextual conditioning of the word in many experiences; some of which were real life experiences and others were those recorded in Scripture. New Testament vocabulary can be developed primarily in this way. One can make a word like *Goti* and condition it to mean *God* by surrounding it with sufficient contexts that cause it to mean exactly that. [47]

Another method is to widen the meaning of old words. This happens often in languages. The Swahili speaking people of east Africa never knew what an airplane or an airport was until they were introduced to them. Therefore, they never had a word for airport. So, now an airport is "uwanja wa ndege." These words literally mean "a field of birds." If the people can be made to understand a concept, such as the concept of God, they themselves may suggest the word or combination of words to use.

We have already seen that Theos had a pagan background. Kurios also had pagan associations. The ultimate "lord" in the Roman Empire was Caesar. He was considered to be a god. Refusing to accept this was one of the things that got Christians in trouble. The New Testament and the preaching of the gospel declared Jesus Christ to be the Lord of all, king of kings and Lord of lords. Eventually it was the New Testament view that prevailed.

Dr. Turner describes how this worked out with the Kaka people of Cameroon, who had a god named Ndjambie.

They considered *Ndjambie* to be a venerated spider that, having spun the web that supports the universe, became submerged in the universe and lost all interest in it. He was not immoral, but amoral. He did not care about whether people did right or wrong and was the epitome of unpredictable fate. How is it possible that such a word as *Ndjambie* could ever be used to represent the God of the universe? The process of development went like this:

(1) The missionaries learned the Kaka culture in order to understand what *Ndjambie* meant to the people. This gave them a basis for making changes in the people's concept of God.

(2) The missionaries used the word *Ndjambie* in many biblical contexts. The things said about *Ndjambie* in these new contexts caused this word to take on new meanings. By teaching history as recorded in Scripture, but using the word Ndjambie in the places where God is mentioned, the people began to realize that he was not a cosmic spider who had spun the universe, but a loving person who had created the world and mankind.[48]

Conclusion

The method we should use to translate the name of God is clear. The foundation of our understanding was laid by God Himself when He chose to translate His Hebrew name, Elohim, into Greek as Theos and His great name Jehovah into Greek as Kurios. This reveals that it is not His plan to *transliterate* the name of Jehovah into other languages. Instead, He has chosen to have many names in many languages. God Himself is the cause of the more than 7,000 languages that exist on earth. He confused the languages at Babel. Since it is not His will that all nations speak the same language, it is not His will that all nations speak Hebrew. So, His Hebrew name should not be transliterated into other languages, except in those few places the KJV did it (Exodus 6:3; Psalms 83:18; Isaiah 12:2; Isaiah 26:4), so that all will know what that name is.

In many languages God has placed a word for God that He seems pleased to use. There are words in various languages that closely match the meaning of Kurios. These words are well suited to use for Jehovah and the Lord Jesus Christ. When a missionary cannot find a word for God or Lord in the mother tongue, there are ways to combine or create words that can be used. However, these will most likely need to be conditioned through Bible translation and teaching.

Chapter Four
Should Δοῦλος (Doulos) be translated Servant or Slave

Paul and Timotheus, the servants of Jesus Christ (Phil. 1:1)

According to the LSB preface, δοῦλος (doulos), should be consistently translated "slave" throughout the New Testament. The KJV translated the term as servant, bond, and bondman. John MacArthur and the LSB translators believe that it is incorrect and inconsistent to translate the Greek word as "servant." They explain their reasoning in their preface.

> **The Terminology of Slave:** The NASB has already translated the Greek term doulos frequently as "slave" in the NT. The LSB made this consistent across the NT. This upholds the lexical definition of the term, its consistent translation, and its distinction from other terms that do denote a "servant." Such consistency also highlights a biblical theological reality that Christians were slaves of sin but now are slaves of Christ (Rom 6:16–22). Biblical writers did not shy from this term because it condemned a wicked form of slavery (i.e., to sin, Satan, and death), highlighted the power of redemption, and affirmed one's total submission to the lordship of Christ. [49]

When someone makes a statement that is contrary to what we have been taught or is different from what we are used to, we should not simply accept what is said without some study and thought. In fact, it is best not to accept anything that is not well proved from Scripture. The statement above makes several points, but it has very little scripture to prove the points. Remember, too, that there are sometimes limitations to lexical definitions of Greek words. One should always be aware of how words are used in biblical contexts. Lexicons most often give the basic definitions, but words are often used in ways that are not consistent with basic definitions. An example of this is the word *cat*. the basic definition of cat is a feline creature. However, that is not what is meant when a man is called a "cool cat" (a good jazz player).

So what shall we do? First, we need to get some definitions of both the Greek and English words. Secondly, we need to know the customs of slavery as practiced in the Roman Empire. Then, we will investigate what the Scriptures of the New Testament say about slavery and about being servants of Christ. Finally, we will come to some conclusions.

Definitions

We will begin with definitions of the Greek word, doulos. First, we look at definitions from two more recent lexicons: The Word Study Dictionary (1992) and Mounce Concise Greek-English Dictionary (1993). This will be followed by five older lexicons: Strong's Hebrew and Greek Dictionaries (1890), Thayer's Greek Definitions (1889), A Greek-English Lexicon to the New Testament (Packhurst-1813), A Greek Lexicon Adapted to the New Testament (Loveland-1828), and A New Greek and English Lexicon (Donnegan-1833).

> **1) Mounce:** "a male slave, or servant, of various degrees, Mat_8:9, et al. freq.; a servitor, person of mean condition, Php_2:7; fem. δούλη, a female slave; a handmaiden, Luk_1:38; Luk_1:48; Act_2:18; δοῦλος, used figuratively, in a bad sense, one involved in moral or spiritual thraldom, Joh_8:34; Rom_6:17; Rom_6:20; 1Co_7:23; 2Pe_2:19; in a good sense, a devoted servant or minister, Act_16:17; Rom_1:1; one pledged or bound to serve, 1Co_7:22; 2Co_4:5 [50]
>
> **2) Word Study:** "masc. noun. A slave, one who is in a permanent relation of servitude to another, his will being altogether consumed in the will of the other ... Generally one serving, bound to serve, in bondage ...
>
> > I) A slave, servant, spoken of involuntary service, e.g., a slave as opposed to a free man ... Also generally a servant ...
> >
> > (II) Metaphorically spoken of voluntary service, a servant, implying obedience, devotion ... Implying modesty ...; in praise of modesty .... Spoken of the true followers and

worshipers of God, e.g., a servant of God, either of agents sent from God, as Moses ... or prophets ... or simply of the worshipers of God ... the followers and ministers of Christ ... especially applied to the Apostles ... Used instead of the personal pron. in the oriental style of addressing a superior ... In respect of things, one such as the servant of sin who indulges in or is addicted to something ...

(III) In the sense of minister, attendant, spoken of the officers of an oriental court" [51]

3) Strong's: "a *slave* (literally or figuratively, involuntarily or voluntarily; frequently therefore in a qualified sense of *subjection* or *subserviency*)" [52]

4) Thayer's:

"1) a slave, bondman, man of servile condition

    1a) a slave

    1b) metaphorically, one who gives himself up to another's will those whose service is used by Christ in extending and advancing his cause among men

    1c) devoted to another to the disregard of one's own interests

2) a servant, attendant" [53]

5) Packhurst:

I One in a servile state, a servant or slave

II Christ as a servant

III A servant of God who declares His will

IV A servant of God who worships, serves, and obeys Him [54]

6) Loveland: "a servant, a slave" [55]

7) Donnegan: "a slave; a servant as opposed to ... a master – a subject, of a monarch, or of a conquered state" [56]

Here are seven Greek lexicons (a lexicon is a dictionary) spanning a period of 180 years, 1813 to 1993. Only one of them (Strong's) defines doulos as exclusively a slave. The rest define doulos as a slave *OR* a servant of various kinds, making a distinction between a slave and a servant.

Next, let's look at the definitions of the English terms, *servant* and *slave*. Since the criticism most often falls on the King James Version, we will look at the 1828 Edition of the Wester Dictionary because its definitions are often closer to those followed by the KJV translators.

> **Slave:** 1. A person who is wholly subject to the will of another; one who has no will of his own, but whose person and services are wholly under the control of another.
> 2. One who has lost the poser of resistance; or one who surrenders himself to any power whatever; as a slave to passion, to lust, to ambition.

> **Servant:** 1. A person, male or female, that attends another for the pupose of performing menial offices for him, who is employed by another for such offices or for other labor, and is subject to his command. The word is correlative to master. *Servant differs from slave, as the servant's subjection to a master is voluntary, the slave's is not. Every slave is a servant, but every servant is not a slave.* (emphasis – author's)
> 2. One in a state of subjection.
> 3. In Scripture (Old Testament-Author), a slave; a bondman; one purchased for money, and who was compelled to serve till the year of jubilee; also, one purchased for a term of years.
> 4. The subject of a king; as the servants of David or of Saul. The Syrians became servants to David. 2 Sam 8.
> 5. A person who voluntarily serves another or acts as his minister; as joshua was the servant of Moses, and the apostles the servants of Christ. So Christ himself is called a servant, Isa 42. Moses is called the servant of the Lord, Duet. 34.
> 6. A person employed or used as an instrument in accomplishing God's purposes of mercy or wrath. So Nebuchadnezzar is called the servant of God. Jer 25.
> 7. One who yields obedience to another. The saints are called servants of God, or of righteousness; and the wicked are called the servants of sin. [57]

The definitions above also make it clear that there is a difference between a slave and a servant. The key statement is, "Servant differs from slave, as the servant's subjection to a master is voluntary, the slave's is not. Every slave is a servant, but every servant is not a slave." It also make it clear that some servants are slaves and some are not. The key difference is this, *the servant's subjection to a master is voluntary, the slave's is not.* Keep that in mind. It will be important later.

Slavery in the Roman Empire

The term slave is defined above as one who is wholly subject to the will of another. The use of doulos in the New Testament stands in the historical context of slavery in the Roman Empire. You should be aware of that context. John Pakhurst gave a description of Greco-Roman slavery in his lexicon.

> Of the wretched condition of slaves, according to the laws and customs of the Romans, a late learned writer gives the following delineation. "The common lot of *slaves in general,* says he, was, with the ancients, very deplorable. Of their situation take the following instances: They were held pro nullis, pro mortuis, pro quadrupedibus, *for no men, for dead men, for beasts*; nay, were in a *much worse* state than any cattle whatever – They had no head in the state, no name, tribe, or register. – They were *not capable of being injured*; nor could they take by purchase or descent; had no heirs and therefore could make no will of course. Exclusive of what was called their *peculium*[58], whatever they acquired was their master's: they could not plead or be pleaded, but were *excluded from all civil concerns whatsoever*; - were not entitled to the rights and considerations of *matrimony*, and therefore had no relief in case of adultery; nor were they proper objects of *cognation*[59] or *affinity*[60]; they could be *sold, transferred,* or *pawned* as goods, or personal estate; for goods they were and such were they esteemed; - might be tortured for evidence; punished at the discretion of their lord, and even *put to death* by his authority; together with *many other civil incapacities*, which I have not room to enumerate." [61]

This was the condition of slaves in the Roman Empire. Add to that the fact that they were not slaves by their own choice. They were bought, sold, or taken in war. They had no will of their own and no control whatever over their circumstances. They had no legal rights at all. So, when the word *doulos* is used of a slave in the New Testament, this is what came to mind. This is what the word meant regarding slavery. Slave masters who became Christians were not told in the New Testament to free their slaves, but they were given new standards of conduct toward their slaves.

> 8 *Knowing that whatsoever good thing any man doeth, the same shall he receive of the Lord, whether he be bond or free.*
>
> 9 *And, ye masters, do the same things unto them, forbearing threatening: knowing that your Master also is in heaven; neither is there respect of persons with him.* (Ephesians 6:8-9)

> *Masters, give unto your servants that which is just and equal; knowing that ye also have a Master in heaven.* (Col. 4:1)

On the other hand, slaves were told to remain slaves after getting saved unless they have an opportunity to be free.

> 21 *Art thou called being a servant? care not for it: but if thou mayest be made free, use it rather.*
>
> 22 *For he that is called in the Lord, being a servant, is the Lord's freeman: likewise also he that is called, being free, is Christ's servant.* (1 Cor. 7:21-22)

What Saith the Scriptures?

So, far we have seen that the lexicons do not restrict the meaning of the term *doulos* to slavery only. The term includes the idea of servitude without being a slave. The English term servant also includes both slaves and voluntary servants. What do the Scriptures say? We know that the term is used of slaves in the Roman sense. this can be found in Ephesians 6:8-9; Colossians 4:1; and 1 Cor. 7:21-22. But, is *doulos* used in any other way in the New Testament? Let's look at several passages that will answer this question.

> **Matthew 18:23-30** *Therefore is the kingdom of heaven likened unto a certain king, which would take account of his* **servants.** *24 And when he had begun to reckon, one was brought unto him, which owed him ten thousand talents. 25 But forasmuch as he had not to pay, his lord commanded him to be sold, and his wife, and children, and all that he had, and payment to be made. 26 The servant therefore fell down, and worshipped him, saying, Lord, have patience with me, and I will pay thee all. 27 Then the lord of that servant was moved with compassion, and loosed him, and forgave him the debt. 28 But the same servant went out, and found one of his fellowservants, which owed him an hundred pence: and he laid hands on him, and took him by the throat, saying, Pay me that thou owest. 29 And his fellowservant fell down at his feet, and besought him, saying, Have patience with me, and I will pay thee all. 30 And he would not: but went and cast him into prison, till he should pay the debt.*

This parable was given to emphasize the importance of forgiveness. Nevertheless, it has some implications for the meaning of the word *doulos*. Several things are worthy of notice in that regard. First, the servant owed the king ten thousand talents. That has been estimated to be at least two million English pounds in about 1890. [62] Considering the laws of slavery in the Roman Empire, how could a slave have a debt such as this? It is understood that the point of this parable is to show how great a debt the King forgives compared to the small debt the forgiven servant would not forgive. However, the parables of the Lord Jesus are usually based on reality. Notice that the servant not only owes an impossible debt, but he has power to cast a fellow servant into prison. This all seems inconsistent with Roman slavery. It has been suggested that the servant with the large debt is most likely a regional governor serving under the King and no slave at all, even though he is a *doulos*.

> **Matthew 20:26-28** *But it shall not be so among you: but whosoever will be great among you, let him be your **minister**; 27 And whosoever will be chief among you, let him be your **servant**: 28 Even as the Son of man came not to be **ministered** unto, but to **minister**, and to give his life a ransom for many.*

The word for servant in these verses is *doulos*. Do these verses really say that to be a leader in the Christian community, you have to become a *slave* to everyone else? Of course, the verses aren't saying that. In fact, the word *servant* in verse 27 is defined by the word *minister* in verse 26 and *to minister* in verse 28. If you want to be great or chief, be a minister, that is, a servant, because Jesus is our example, who was a minister. A servant is a minister, because Jesus came to minister. The term servant is defined as a minister. The word *servant* is used as a *synonym* of *minister*. The word translated *minister* is *diakonos*. Therefore, *doulos* is a *synonym* of *diakonos*. The word *diakonos* is consistently defined in the Greek lexicons listed above as to *serve the needs of others*. It is *never* defined as *slave* and never *means* slave. The same is seen in Mark 10:43-45.

> **Philippians 2:5-8** Let this mind be in you, which was also in Christ Jesus: 6 Who, being in the form of God, thought it not robbery to be equal with God: 7 But made himself of no reputation, and took upon him the form of a **servant**, and was made in the likeness of men: 8 And being found in fashion as a man, he humbled himself, and became obedient unto death, even the death of the cross.

The LSB translated *doulos* in these verses as *slave* rather than servant, as translated in the KJV. But, was Jesus in the form of a *slave*? Go back and review the description of a Roman slave. Is that Jesus? Is that the kind of life He lived? He came to live the life of a servant, but not as a Roman slave. It is ridiculous and an insult to the Lord Jesus Christ to say so. What kind of a *doulos* was Jesus? The answer to that question is simple. He was a *diakonos*, a minister, a servant. He said so Himself in Matthew 20:26-28, quoted above, *"Even as the Son of man came not to be **ministered** unto, but to **minister**, and to give his life a ransom for many."* Philippians 2 says that He is a *doulos* and Matthew 20 *defines* it as a *diakonos*, a servant. Doulos certainly means slave in certain contexts, but in other contexts it means servant.

> **2 Corinthians 4:5** For we preach not ourselves, but Christ Jesus the Lord; and ourselves your **servants** for Jesus' sake.

The Greek word for *servants* in this verse is *doulos*. Is it possible that Paul and his fellow servants were *slaves* to all the Corinthian believers, as the LSB says? I think Paul would laugh at that. When *doulos* is used for slavery, it means real slavery. Was that really Paul's position with the Corinthians? Certainly not! He was a servant, in that he sought their good (as a *minister* does), but he was not a slave. Once again, this shows that *doulos* does not exclusively mean *slave*. It is also a non-slave servant.

An example of a context in which doulos is clearly referring to slavery is Galatians 3:28.

> **Gal 3:28** There is neither Jew nor Greek, there is neither **bond** nor free, there is neither male nor female: for ye are all one in Christ Jesus.

The word *bond* is translated from *Doulos* and is clearly referring to slavery. So, a person who is a slave is *bound* to another human, not free. That would certainly not apply to the Lord Jesus Christ or to Paul in his service to the Corinthians, or to us, the Lord's servants.

Is a Christian Servant a Slave?

As we already know, some servants are slaves and some are not. There are distinct differences between the two. As I noted above, Webster's dictionary, 1828 Edition, said, "Servant differs from slave, as the servant's subjection to a master is voluntary, the slave's is not." When one reviews the conditions of a Christian servant as opposed to the condition of a slave, other differences also come to light.

1) The Christian's service is voluntary, not forced:

Rom 6:12-13 Let not sin therefore reign in your mortal body, that ye should obey it in the lusts thereof. 13 Neither yield ye your members as instruments of unrighteousness unto sin: but yield yourselves unto God, as those that are alive from the dead, and your members as instruments of righteousness unto God.

Christians are not forced to yield, but they are to voluntarily yield to God and righteousness.

Romans 12:1 I beseech you therefore, brethren, by the mercies of God, that ye present your bodies a living sacrifice, holy, acceptable unto God, which is your reasonable service.

If Christians were slaves, they would be forced to do this. Instead, they are begged to do it voluntarily. The kind of dedication described in this verse only happens by choice.

2) The Christian's service results in reward

1 Corinthians 3:11-15 For other foundation can no man lay than that is laid, which is Jesus Christ. 12 Now if any man build upon this foundation gold, silver, precious stones, wood, hay, stubble; 13 Every man's work shall be made manifest: for the day shall declare it, because it shall be revealed by fire; and the fire shall try every man's work of what sort it is. 14 If any man's work abide which he hath built thereupon, he shall receive a reward. 15 If any man's work shall be burned, he shall suffer loss: but he himself shall be saved; yet so as by fire.

2 Corinthians 5:10 For we must all appear before the judgment seat of Christ; that every one may receive the things done in his body, according to that he hath done, whether it be good or bad.

Slaves are not paid for their labor. They must labor or be punished. Christians are rewarded for labor done according to the will of God.

3) The Christian's service and obedience results in reigning with Christ.

2 Timothy 2:12 If we suffer, we shall also reign with him: if we deny him, he also will deny us:
2 Timothy 3:12 Yea, and all that will live godly in Christ Jesus shall suffer persecution.
Part of the responsibility of a slave is utter obedience. The same is required for a Christian servant. However, no slave is ever given the opportunity to become a king. All Christians are given that opportunity. This makes Christian service fundamentally different than slavery.

4) The Christian is not a slave but is a member of the family.

Romans 8:14-15 For as many as are led by the Spirit of God, they are the sons of God. 15 For ye have not received the spirit of bondage again to fear; but ye have received the Spirit of adoption, whereby we cry, Abba, Father. 16 The Spirit itself beareth witness with our spirit, that we are the children of God:
Sometimes Roman slaves were adopted into a family, but not until they were freed. Christians are members of God's family. They are children of God. Therefore, Christians are not slaves, rather, they are true servants, but still free.

5) The Christian is not a slave, he is an heir of God.

Romans 8:17 And if children, then heirs; heirs of God, and joint-heirs with Christ; if so be that we suffer with him, that we may be also glorified together.

Remember, no slave was an heir of his master. This is another reason to believe that the Christian servant is not a slave, but a true, voluntary, and committed servant of Christ.

Conclusions

So, what have we discovered? First, regarding definitions, we have found that the definitions of the Greek word *doulos* are two: slave and servant. The definitions of the English word servant, according to the Webster 1828, is the same: *Servant differs from slave, as the servant's subjection to a master is voluntary, the slave's is not. Every slave is a servant, but every servant is not a slave.*

These two definitions are also confirmed in the way doulos is used in the Scriptures. *Doulos* is shown to be the word used for a servant of a king (Matthew 18:23-30), a *doulos* who was probably a regional governor. The word *doulos* is also used as a synonym of the word *diakonos*, which can only be a servant and not a slave (Matthew 20:26-28). In the KJV, this means the servant is a *synonym* of minister. Jesus was a *doulos* (Phil. 2:5-8) in the sense of being a minister (Matt. 20:26-28). Paul's example shows that the term *doulos* does not always mean slave (2 Corinthians 4:5).

Therefore, the Christian servant is not a slave. The believer voluntarily commits himself to obedient service (Romans 12:1). He is not forced into slavery. Unlike a slave, the service of a Christian is richly rewarded (1 Corinthians 3:11-15). Also, unlike a slave, faithful Christian service and obedience result in ruling and reigning with Christ in the Millennium (2 Timothy 2:12). Rather than being a slave, the believer is a member of God's family (Romans 8:14-15) and is, therefore, an heir of God (Romans 8:17).

John MacArthur and the LSB translators insist that the only correct way translate *doulos* is *slave*. Furthermore, they insist that *doulos* must be translated *slave* every time it is used. In contrast, the KJV translators rendered doulos as *servant* nearly every time it was used. In a few cases, the KJV has translated it *bond* or *bondman*. The KJV translators were aware that *doulos* did not always mean slave, but that sometimes it also meant a non-slave servant. They were also aware that the English word *servant* also carried both meanings. It was doubtless the leading of God that caused them to translate *doulos* as *servant* in the great majority of its appearances in the New Testament. By doing that, they allowed the context of each passage to determine whether it meant a slave servant or a non-slave servant.

About the Author

Dr. Steve Combs is an ordained minister. He spent his early years in Kentucky, Virginia, and finally Ohio. He was not raised in a Christian home. He had some Christian influence from his grandmother, but that had little effect on him. Due to discussions with a Baptist preacher and a Sunday School teacher, who visited his home, he began to read the Bible. The Word of God had its effect. He came under strong conviction of his sins. A friend invited him to a nearby church during revival meetings, where he heard the gospel preached.

God showed him that Jesus Christ, the Son of God, paid for his sins when he died on the cross and, afterward, rose physically from the dead. He believed it with all his heart and, as a result, he was born spiritually into the family of God and saved from condemnation for his sins.

Since then there have been major transformations to his life. God called him to preach and enabled a backward shy individual suffering from an inferiority complex to stand before crowds and confidently proclaim the Word of God. God gave him a business background as a CPA and God put him in several ministry positions. He has served as a Bible Institute teacher and Dean, a youth pastor, assistant pastor, and a senior pastor. He holds a Doctor of Theology from Covington Theological Seminary.

Currently Steve Combs is Assistant Director and a Global Translation Advisor for Bearing Precious Seed Global/ Global Bible Translators, www.bpsglobal.com. BPS Global starts and assists Bible translation projects around the world.

He is married and has four married children.

Notes

[1] Wikipedia article on John MacArthur. Nov. 2021

[2] John MacArthur, Mid-Week Message to Grace Community Church, April 2020, You Tube. Web. Nov 2021. Linked and quoted on Duncan Johnson blog. https://duncanjohnson.ca/blog/2020/04/02/macarthur-legacy-standard-bible. Web.

[3] Legacy Standard Bible Web Site. https://lsbible.org/origin. Nov. 2021.

[4] LSB, *PREFACE TO THE LEGACY STANDARD BIBLE.* https://lsbible.org/preface. Web. Nov, 2021.

[5] Preface.

[6] The Official Biblia Hebraica web site. Deutsche Biblia Gesellschaft. https://www.academic-bible.com/en/bible-society-and-biblical-studies/scholarly-editions/hebrew-bible/bhk. Web. Nov. 2021

[7] Wikipedia. Biblia Hebraica (Kittel). 2021. https://en.wikipedia.org/wiki/Biblia_Hebraica_(Kittel). Web. Dec. 2021.

[8] United Bible Societies. http://ubs-translations.org/ cat/biblical_texts/ greek_scriptures_and_reference/new_testament. Web. Dec 2021.

[9] Fowler, Everette W. *Evaluating Versions of the New Testament.* (Watertown, WI: Maranatha Baptist Press, 1981) p. 28-66. Print. 19 August 2014.

[10] Thayer, Joseph Henry. *Thayer's Greek Definitions.* 1889. Included in E-sword.net free Bible software download, copyright 2000-2019.

[11] Strong, James. *Strong's Hebrew and Greek Dictionaries.* 1890. Included in E-sword.net free Bible software download, copyright 2000-2019. Web.

[12] I hope the reader will pardon me if I do not spell out the name this cult calls itself. When a heretical cult calls itself by God's great name of Jehovah, I feel I am taking His name in vain if I use it in identifying them. They are *not* witnesses for Jehovah.

[13] LSB. *Preface.*

[14] LSB. *Preface.*

[15] User Jb344tul. Wikipedia. Photo of Great Isaiah Scroll facsimile, showing columns 12-13 (chapter 14-16). Licensed under Creative Commons CC0 1.0 Universal Public Domain Dedication. Accessed 2022.

[16] Istanbul Archaeology Museum. Gezer calendar close up.jpg. Wikipedia. Licensed under the Creative Commons Attribution-Share Alike 3.0 Unported license. Link to license: https://creativecommons.org/licenses/by-sa/3.0/deed.en. Photo changed to grayscale. Accessed Apr. 2022.

[17] Wilson, Dr. Ralph F. Bible Studies. http://www.jesuswalk.com/names-god. Web. Dec. 2021.

[18] Yahweh's Assembly in Yahshua. *Is His Name Jehovah or Yahweh?* 2963 County Road 233, Kingdom City, Missouri 65262. 2007. www.YAIY.org. Web. Dec. 2021.

[19] Parsons, John L. *Hebrew Names of God*. Hebrew4Christians. Web. Dec. 2021

[20] Parsons

[21] LSB. *Preface.*

[22] Wikipedia. Leningrad Manuscript. picture by Shmuel ben Ya'akov. Published in Wikipedia. Public Domain. Accessed Dec. 2021.

[23] Aleppo Codex, Closeup of Aleppo Codex, Joshua 1:1 in Hebrew, scanned by http://www.aleppocodex.org. Public Domain. Published in Wikipedia. Accessed Dec. 2021.

[24] Evidence from the Aleppo Manuscript. SeekingTruth.info. Web. Dec. 2021.

[25] *Evidence …*

[26] Religious News LLC. *The original Hebrew name of God Re-discovered in 1,000 Bible manuscripts.* https://religionnews.com/2018/01/25/the-original-hebrew-name-of-god-re-discovered-in-1000-bible-manuscripts/#:~:text=The%20project%20to%20find%20new%20evidence%20corroborating%20this,Bible%20manuscripts%20with%20vowels%2C%20Russian%20National%20Library%2C%20Evr. Jan. 25, 218, Web, Dec. 2021.

[27] Religious News LLC. *The original Hebrew name of God re-discovered in 1,000 Bible manuscripts*

[28] Hebrew Today. *The Hebrew Alphabet -The Letter Vav (ו) In the Hebrew Alphabet.* The Letter Vav (ו) In the Hebrew Alphabet - Hebrew Today. Hebrew Today is a publication house based in Jerusalem. Web. Dec. 2021.

[29] Navah. *How to Utter Hebrew Vav: "Vav" or "Waw?* https://timeofreckoning.org. Web. Dec. 2021.

[30] Ben Tziyyon. Vav vs. Waw. Virtual Yashiva Discussion Forum. www.tapatalk.com. 2021. Web. Dec. 2021.

[31] Strong

[32] Nehemia Gordon. Cited. Nathan Lawrence. *The Name of the Creator and How NOT to Pronounce It. https://hoshanarabbah.org/blog/2017/01/19/name-of-the-creator.* Web. accessed Dec. 2021.

[33] Nehemia Gordaon. cited by Lawrence.

[34] LSB, Preface.

[35] Churchunity.net. *Yahweh, Jupiter of the Hosts (18th Century A.D.).* Web. Accessed Dec. 2021.

[36] Wilhelm Gesenius. *Gesenius's Hebrew and Chaldee Lexicon to the Old Testament Scriptures.* Translated with Additions and Corrections from the Author's Thesaurus and Other Works, by Samuel Prideax Tregelles. London:

Samuel Bagster and Sons. Pg 337. Digitized by the Internet Archive funded by Microsoft. https://archive.org/details/hebrewchaldeelex00geseuoft/ page/n5/mode/1up?view=theater. Web. Accessed Dec. 2021.

[37] Flavius Josephus, *Antiquities of the Jews.* Book 12, Chapter 5. (c. 94 AD) Included in E-sword.net free Bible software download, copyright 2000-2019. Web. Dec. 2021.

[38] Don Richardson. Eternity in Their Hearts. Regal Books: Ventura, Ca. 1981. Print. pp. 9-20.

[39] Richardson, pp 41-47

[40] Richardson, pp. 54-56

[41] Richardson, pp. 56-59

[42] Wikipedia

[43] Wikipedia and The English Kikuyu Bible found on Google Play. Homegrown Devs. 2022

[44] This information comes partly from Wikipedia and partly from David Misiko, a member of the Busuku tribe.

[45] Denis Okoth. *Communicating Christ Among Folk Religionists, Kingdom Ministry in Satan's Nest/ Luo Animistic Beliefs and Religious Practitioners and How to Reconcile Them to Christ.* Missology.org. Web. 2022.

[46] Noah Wester. *Webster's Dictionary, 1828 Edition.* Included in E-sword.net free Bible software download, copyright 2000-2019. Web.

[47] Charles Turner, *Biblical Bible Translating*, Sovereign Grace Publishers, Inc: Layfayette, In. 2001. Google Books Edition.

[48] Turner

[49] LSB preface

[50] William D. Mounce. *Mounce's Concise English-Greek Lexicon.* 1993. Included in E-sword.net free Bible software download, copyright 2000-2019. Web.

[51] Spiros Zodhiates, Warren Baker, and Gene Carpenter. *The Complete Word Study Dictionary.* AMG, International, Inc.. 1993. Included in E-sword.net free Bible software download, copyright 2000-2019. Web.

[52] James Strong. *Strong's Hebrew and Greek Dictionaries.* 1890. Included in E-sword.net free Bible software download, copyright 2000-2019. Web.

[53] Joseph H. Thayer. *Thayer's Greek Definitions.* 1889. Included in E-sword.net free Bible software download, copyright 2000-2019. Web.

[54] John Pakhurst. *A Greek and English Lexicon to the New Testament.* Thomas Turnbull: Edinburgh. 1813.

[55] Samuel Loveland. *A Greek Lexicon Adapted to the New Testament.* David Watson: Woodstock, Vt. 1828. Google Books Edition.

[56] James Donnegan. *A New Greek and English Lexicon.* Hilliard Gray and Co: Boston; G & C & H Carville: New York. 1833. Google Books Edition.

[57] Daniel Webster. Webster's Dictionary of American English (1828). Included in E-sword.net free Bible software download, copyright 2000-2019. Web.

[58] Noun **peculium** (plural peculia) (law, historical) The savings of a son or a slave, with the father 's or master 's consent; a little property or stock of one's own. https://en.wiktionary.org/wiki/peculium

[59] Webster, 1828: Kindred; relation by descent from the same original.

[60] Webster, 1828: The relation contracted by marriage, between a husband and his wife's kindred, and between a wife and her husband's kindred; in contradistinction from consanguinity or relation by blood.

[61] Pakhurst. citing: Dr. John Taylor. *Elements of Civil Law.* pp. 428, 429.

[62] The Preachers Complete Homiletical Commentary. 1892. Included in E-sword.net free Bible software download, copyright 2000-2019. Web.